MACROECONOMICS
THEORIES AND POLICIES

Dr. Rajesh Gade
Dr. Avinash Hande
Dr. Vikas Barbate
Dr. Vinodkumar Pathade

BLUEROSE PUBLISHERS
India | U.K.

Copyright © Dr Rajesh Gade, Dr Avinash Hande, Dr Vikas Barbate, Prof. Vinodkumar Pathade 2023

All rights reserved by author. No part of this publication may be reproduced, stored in a retrieval system or transmitted in any form or by any means, electronic, mechanical, photocopying, recording or otherwise, without the prior permission of the author. Although every precaution has been taken to verify the accuracy of the information contained herein, the publisher assume no responsibility for any errors or omissions. No liability is assumed for damages that may result from the use of information contained within.

BlueRose Publishers takes no responsibility for any damages, losses, or liabilities that may arise from the use or misuse of the information, products, or services provided in this publication.

For permissions requests or inquiries regarding this publication,
please contact:

BLUEROSE PUBLISHERS
www.BlueRoseONE.com
info@bluerosepublishers.com
+91 8882 898 898
+4407342408967

ISBN: 978-93-5668-639-7

Cover design: Muskan Sachdeva
Typesetting: Pooja Sharma

First Edition: July 2023

Preface

Macroeconomics: Theories and Policies examine and analyses the performance of the economy as a whole. Macroeconomics is the branch of economics that deals with the study of the economy as a whole, including national income, employment, inflation, and monetary policy. It plays a critical role in shaping the economic policies of governments, central banks, and other institutions around the world. The aim of this book is to provide an in-depth understanding of the various concepts and theories of macroeconomics.

The book is divided into ninth chapters, each of which covers a different aspect of macroeconomics. Chapter first provides an introduction to the subject, including its definition, nature, scope, and importance. Chapter second deals with the measurement of national income, including the various concepts and methods used for its estimation. Chapter third focuses on the theories of output and employment, including the classical and Keynesian approaches.

Chapter fourth delves into the demand for money, covering different schools of thought such as the classical, neo-classical, Keynesian, and Friedman approaches. Chapter fifth discusses the supply of money and the instruments of monetary control, including the role of the Reserve Bank of India (RBI) in controlling the money supply.

Chapter six explores the dynamic aspects of macroeconomics, including the wage-employment relationship, wage and price stickiness, and the Phillips curve. Chapter seven focus on inflation and its relationship with money, covering topics such as the Phillips curve, the non-accelerating inflation rate of unemployment (NAIRU), and economic policies to control inflation.

Chapter eight examines the budget constraint and the financing of budget deficits, including the concepts of money financing and debt financing. It also covers the Ricardian equivalence and its view on debt financing of budget deficits. Chapter nine cover various aspects of Behavioural economics and its relationship with Macro Economics. It also covers biases in Behavioural economics. And finally Chapter ten includes few caselet of Macro Economics.

In writing this book, we have benefited immensely from various websites, books, journals and magazines. We are grateful to all of them. We also express our deep sense of gratitude to friend and family members of Dr.Rajesh, Dr.Avinash, Dr.Vikas and Dr. Vinodkumar. We are deeply grateful to the publisher for bringing out this book on time. Suggestions are welcome from all and will be thankfully acknowledged.

Contents

Chapter 1: Introduction to Macroeconomics 1

    1.1. Introduction 1

    1.2. Definitions of Macroeconomics: 2

    1.3. Nature of Macroeconomics: 3

    1.4. Scope of Macroeconomics: 5

    1.5. Importance of Macroeconomics: 10

    1.6. Limitations of macroeconomics: 12

    1.7. Difference between Microeconomics and Macroeconomics ...14

    1.8. Objectives of Macroeconomic: 16

    1.9. Questions 20

Chapter 2: National Income 21

    2.1. Meaning: 21

    2.2. Definitions of National Income: 22

    2.3. Concepts of National Income. 24

    2.4. Circular flow of income. 34

    2.5. Measurement of National Income: 38

    2.6. Importance of National Income Analysis. 40

    2.7. Difficulties in the measurement of national income: 42

    2.8. Questions: 45

Chapter 3: Theories of Output and Employment 46

    3.1. Introduction: 46

    3.2. The classical theory of employment: 47

    3.3. The Say's Law: 52

    3.4. JM Keynes' criticisms of the classical theories: 56

   3.5. Keynes theory of employment: 59

   3.6. Questions: 71

Chapter 4: Demand for money 72

   4.1. Classical approach to demand for money 72

   4.2. Cambridge approach or the neoclassical approach to demand
        for money. 74

   4.3. Keynesian approach to demand for money... 74

   4.4. Friedman's approach to demand for money 80

   4.5. Tobin's portfolio approach to demand for money 83

   4.6. Baumol's inventory approach to transactions demand for money......... 84

   4.7. Questions: 87

Chapter 5: Supply of Money & Instruments of Monetary Control 88

   5.1. Concept of money supply 88

   5.2. Constituents of money supply. 89

   5.3. Reserve bank of India's approach to the measurement
        of money supply 90

   5.4. Determinants of money supply 91

   5.5. Instruments of monetary control... 93

   5.6. Selective or Qualitative Instruments of Monetary Policy..................... 96

   5.7. Questions 99

Chapter.6: Dynamic Macroeconomics 100

   6.1. Introduction 100

   6.2. Wage-employment relationship.. 100

   6.3. Wage and price stickiness... 104

   6.4. From Phillip's curve to the aggregate supply curve 108

   6.5. Long-run aggregate supply curve 108

   6.6. Questions 109

Chapter 7: Inflation and Money 110

7.1. Introduction 110

7.2. The Phillip's curve 110

7.3. The nairu : the non-accelerating-inflation rate of unemployment. 113

7.4. The long run Philips curve 116

7.5. Economics policies to control inflation 116

7.6. Long-term policies to control inflation 119

7.7. Fisher's equation 121

7.8. Quantity theory of money.. 123

7.9. Inflation tax 125

7.10. Questions 129

Chapter 8: Budget constraint: Money and Debt Financing of Budget Deficits 130

8.1. Introduction 130

8.2. Government budget constraint 131

8.3. Money financing of budget deficit 132

8.4. Printed money and the inflation tax 133

8.5. Debt financing of budget deficit 137

8.6. Wealth Effect of Debt-Financing 139

8.7. Debt-financing of budget deficit: the view of ricardian equivalence ... 141

8.8. Questions 144

Chapter 9: Behavioural Economics and Macro Economics 145

9.1. Meaning and definition 145

9.2. Importance 146

9.3. Key concepts 147

9.4. Advantages of Behavioural Economics 147

9.5. Criticisms 150

9.6. Biases in Behavioural economics 151

9.7. Questions 154

Chapter 10: Caselet 155

10.1. Financial Crises in Yemen... 155

10.2. Financial crisis in Lebanon 156

10.3. Economic crisis in Greece 157

10.4. Economic slowdown in Russia.. 157

10.5. Economic crisis in Zambia 158

10.6. Economic crisis in Suriname 159

10.7. Economic crisis in Sri Lanka... 160

10.8. Conclusion... 162

Chapter 1

Introduction to Macroeconomics

1.1. Introduction

The word macroeconomics contains a prefix which has a Greek origin- "makro" which means large. Macroeconomics is a study that analyses all aggregate indicators and macroeconomic factors that have an impact on the economy. Economic policies and strategies are formed by government and companies by using macroeconomic models. Macroeconomics is the branch of economics that deals with the behaviour and performance of an economy as a whole. Macroeconomics lays more focus on the aggregate changes that happen in a particular economy.

Macroeconomics is not concerned with activities of individuals or the activities of a single firm. It concentrates on the aggregate of individual units for a particular economy. Instead of studying concepts like individual demand or supply, macroeconomics focuses on concepts like aggregate demand and aggregate supply. It deals with concepts like total employment, national income and national growth, national output, total consumption, general price level, interest rates, inflation trade cycles et cetera.

While microeconomics deals with an individual's economic behaviour, macroeconomics deals with aggregate economic behaviour of the citizen. Microeconomics deals with the pricing of a particular commodity in an industry whereas macroeconomics deals with the general price levels that prevail in the economy. It studies concepts like national income national accounting et cetera. The basic parameter of studying microeconomics is price whereas the basic parameter for macroeconomic analysis is income. Microeconomics cannot be completely neglected because it is important for proper utilisation of resources and for making individual business decisions. Macroeconomics is also important as it helps the government to formulate economic policies and generate growth and wealth for the nation. It can be said that microeconomics provides a bottom-up view of the economy whereas macroeconomics shows the top-down view of the economy. The overall objectives of microeconomics are gaining maximum profit for an individual or a firm within the industry. Macroeconomics on the other hand, has bigger objective is that deal with stabilising economies, stabilising price, achieving full employment etc.

The origin of macroeconomics can be traced back to the early 1500s. A Polish mathematician Nicolaus Copernicus formulated the quantity theory of money in the year 1517. The theory states that general price level of goods and services are directly proportional to the amount of money in circulation or the supply of money.

Before the Second World War, the quantity theory of money was extremely influential. Well-known economists like Milton Friedman, Irwing Fisher, and Anna Schwartz made several improvements to the original quantity theory of money. However, John Maynard Keynes strongly criticised the quantity theory of money upon the basis that a direct relationship between the supply of money and price levels cannot be established. Ever since then, several schools of macroeconomic thought have emerged after Keynes published his general theory in the year 1936. In his publication, the subject of macroeconomics was treated as a separate discipline. JM Keynes revolutionised economic thinking and the Keynesian School of macroeconomic thought was born. It considered the demand side of macroeconomic policies.

Later, in the 1960s, several economists challenged the Keynesian approach to macroeconomic thought. They emphasised the importance of monetary policies in bringing about macroeconomic stability. By the mid-1970s, there were dramatic changes to macroeconomic thought. This led to the emergence of a second school of thought which emerged out of the theories related to rational expectations. Therefore, the subject of macroeconomics has evolved through the decades and has gained significant importance in shaping the future of economies.

1.2. Definitions of Macroeconomics:

The Merriam-Webster's dictionary defines macroeconomics as: "a study of economics in terms of whole systems especially with reference to general levels of output and income and to the interrelations among sectors of the economy".

Prof Kenneth E Boulding defines macroeconomics as follows: "Macroeconomics deals, not with individual quantities as such but with the aggregates of these quantities, not with individual incomes but with national income, not with prices but with the price level, not with individual output but with the national output".

According to Prof Gardner Ackley, "Macroeconomics concerns itself with such variables as the aggregate volume of the output of an economy, with the extent to which its resources are employed, with the size of the national income, with the general price level".

According to J.L. Hansen," macroeconomics is that branch of economics which considers the relationship between large, aggregated variables such as the volume of employment, the total amount of savings, investment, national income et cetera."

The Economist's Dictionary of Economics defines macroeconomics as "the study of whole economic system is aggregating over the functioning of individual economic units. It is primarily concerned with the variables which follow systematic and predictable parts of the area and can be analysed independently based on the decisions of many agents who determine their level. More specifically, it is a study of national economies and the determination of national income."

Prof Carl Shapiro - "macroeconomics deals with the functioning of the economy as a whole."

By analysing the above definitions, we can understand that macroeconomics is a study of aggregates. Macroeconomic studies the economic problems from the point of view of the entire economy. It deals with various concepts such as national income, aggregate savings and other agents. It is a study that deals with the averages of the entire system rather than a particular item. It attempts to define these aggregates so that the relationship between such variables can be examined.

1.3. Nature of Macroeconomics:

1. **Macroeconomics is based on the study of aggregates:** Macroeconomics has a wide scope and is concerned with the study of aggregates. It studies aggregate demand, aggregate supply, general price levels, national income, total output and other variables that indicate the condition of the economy as a whole.

2. **Lumping method:** Macroeconomics makes the use of lumping method for the purpose of understanding economic aggregates. By using the lumping method macroeconomic studies, the general price level as against the price

levels of individual products. Unlike microeconomics, macroeconomics does not consider the prices of individual products or services.

3. **The experimental nature of macroeconomics:** According to John Duffy, "Experimental macroeconomics is a subfield of experimental economics that makes use of controlled laboratory methods to understand aggregate economic phenomena and to test the specific assumptions and predictions of macroeconomic models." Therefore, macroeconomics can use laboratory experiments, involving small groups of subjects who interact with each other for short periods of time. Such experiments help researchers to understand, analyse the economy wide phenomena and build economic models or make predictions.

4. **Macroeconomic analysis is statistical in nature:** macroeconomic analysis uses economic trend analysis, long-term macroeconomic projections, analysing the impact of fiscal and monetary measures etc. various macroeconomic models are an essential part of macroeconomic analysis. Various statistical methods and tools are used for the purpose of performing such an analysis. Therefore, statistics plays a major role in shaping the very nature of macroeconomic analysis.

5. **Useful in policy formulation:** with the help of macroeconomic analysis, the government formulate and implement's economic policies. The government achieves control over the developmental aspects of an economy by regulating the different aggregates of the economic system. The final aim of the government is to bring about economic stability in the country. For the purpose of bringing about stabilisation of prices and other economic variables, the government analyses the general price levels, the general level of output, level of employment etc.

6. **Income theory:** Income theory is a body of macroeconomic analysis which is concerned with the relative levels of output, employment, and prices in an economy. The income theory of money was conceived in the 19th century in the first half of the 20th century. It is also called as the income approach to money or the income theory of prices. By defining the interrelationship between different macroeconomic factors, governments try to create policies that can contribute to overall economic stability.

7. **Overall view of the economy:** Macroeconomic analysis provides the governments with the overall view of a particular economy. Various aggregates are interlinked to show the interrelationships between them. By

studying the interrelationships, the governments get a more realistic view of the overall economic condition of the country. The entire process of formulating policies and budgets to bring about development in certain sectors is based on macroeconomic analysis.

1.4. Scope of Macroeconomics:

The study of macroeconomics has a very wide scope. Macroeconomic aggregates affect our daily lives. It studies have an economy operates as a whole. It focuses on different measures such as aggregate demand, aggregate supply and aggregate price level. It studies the way in which these variables are determined and how they change over time. It helps us in understanding various relationships between economic variables and the reasons behind several economic problems. That is why, macroeconomics is also known as the theory of income and employment. It is essential for policymakers to perform macroeconomic analysis for designing different policies at the national level. Macroeconomics also has political importance and helps us understand the current standing of a particular nation in the world. Macroeconomics helps to explain the benefits and challenges of international trade, and how it can contribute to economic development and growth. Macroeconomics provides tools for understanding financial markets, including interest rates, exchange rates, and stock prices, and how they affect economic development.

Macroeconomics provides insights into the causes and consequences of income inequality, and how policies can be developed to promote a more equitable distribution of income. Macroeconomics provides a basis for understanding the relationship between economic growth and the environment, and how policies can be developed to promote sustainable development.

The scope of macroeconomics can be divided into two main categories:

A. Macroeconomic theories.

B. Macroeconomic policies.

A. Macroeconomic theories:

Theories are designed to explain particular phenomena observed by means of a group of rules and underlying basic assumptions. The utility of a particular theory depends upon the capacity to explain and predict the phenomena under study. There are several theories which explain the scope of macroeconomic analysis. They have been discussed as below:

1. **National Income:**

Macroeconomics provides various methods to calculate the national income of a particular country. The scope of macroeconomics extends to various areas related to the measurement and evaluation of national income, expenditure and budgeting. For example, in the financial year 2020, India's per capita net national income or NNI was around ₹ 135,000. The gross national income at constant prices was around ₹ 128 trillion. Macroeconomic analysis of the national income is crucial as it is an important measure of the size of the economy and the level of country's economic performance.

2. **Theories related to flow of money.**

The scope of macroeconomic analysis extends to the functions of the federal banks (RBI in case of India) and their role in the economy. Macroeconomic analysis deals with the measurement of the inflow and outflow of money and its impact on the overall level of employment. For example, macroeconomics deals with measuring foreign currency inflows through indicators like the foreign direct investment (FDI). Foreign direct investments are significant for developing nations and emerging markets where companies need funding and expertise to expand their international sales. FDI inflows in India increased to $55.56 billion in 2015-16, $60.22 billion in 2016-17, $60.97 bn in 2017-18 and the country registered its highest ever FDI inflow of more than $62.00 bn during the Financial Year 2018-19. This happened because in the year 2016, the reserve Bank of India allowed hundred percent.

Figure 1. Scope of macroeconomics

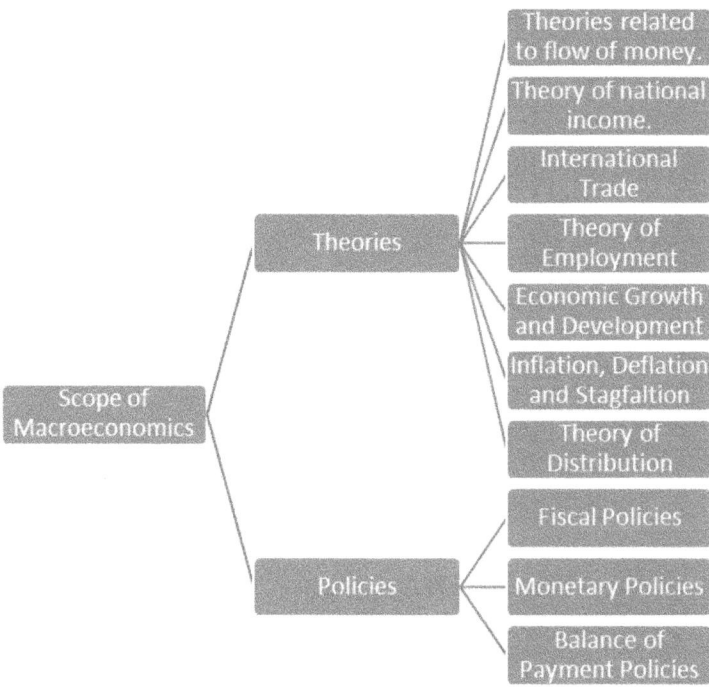

Foreign direct investment through the automatic route to the regulated financial services companies other than banks or insurance companies. It also simplified the rules for easier entry of venture capital funds for start-up ventures. By analysing the foreign direct investments, macroeconomic analysis shows that India is one of the most attractive destinations for foreign direct investments. Macroeconomic analysis also points out that the overall success of the prevailing government in attracting foreign direct investments and creating a long-lasting impact on the economic condition of a particular country.

3. **Theories related to international trade.**

Macroeconomics deals with various indicators of international trade. Studying these indicators is important as it helps in raising the standards of living, providing employment and enabling consumers to enjoy a greater variety of goods. The scope of macroeconomic analysis extends to the international trade patterns and measurement of the impact of globalisation on world trade over several years. For example, while global economy continued to grow and the year

2015, world trade declined by about 10%. Economic indicators showed that there was a decline in the economic interdependence between countries. This shows that the scope of macroeconomics is not only limited to a particular country but can be also extended to the entire world where organisations like United Nations can analyse various key indicators and trends that show changing trends in international trade.

4. **Theory of employment.**

The scope of macroeconomics covers various theories related to employment that helps countries to measure the overall level of employment and its impact on other factors like consumption, savings, expenditure et cetera. Macroeconomics studies 'unemployment rates' which is a percent of the labour force that is jobless in a particular country. For example, Unemployment Rate in India reached an all-time high of 23.50 percent in April of 2020. Therefore, the scope of macroeconomic analysis extends to analysing the (poor) performance of the government in generating employment opportunities.

5. **Economic growth and development.**

The scope of macroeconomic analysis includes measuring and comparing economic growth and development of nations. For example, the overall status of a nation's economy can be measured in terms of per Gross Domestic Product (GDP) per capita. The measure of GDP per capita shows a country's GDP divided by its total population. It is an important indicator of economic performance and is useful for making comparisons of average living standards and economic well-being between economies. For example, in the year 2019 the GDP per capita of India was $ 2013 as compared to $ 56,787 for United States of America.

6. **Inflation, deflation and stagflation:**

The scope of macroeconomics extends to the study of inflationary and deflationary trends in economies. It studies the movements in the consumer price index (CPI). The CPI measures the average change in prices over time that consumers pay for a basket of goods and services. Inflation occurs when the price of the goods and services rise while deflation occurs when those prices decrease. Macroeconomic analysis helps the federal banks of countries to keep a check on the inflationary trends by tweaking the rates of interest, increasing lending rates and taking other measures. Macroeconomics also covers the study of stagflation. Stagflation is a situation in which there is an increase in inflation and a simultaneous stagnation of economic output. Our country has faced six consecutive quarters of slowing growth since the year 2018. In the first quarter of the financial year 2021, consumption demand and investment demand in India contracted by 27% and 47% respectively. Simultaneously, the consumer price index was above 6% for the fifth consecutive month. This shows that that our economy is going into a state of stagflation.

7. Theory of distribution.

The scope of macroeconomics also covers the theories of distribution. These theories are an attempt to account for the sharing of national income among the owners of the factors of production such as land, capital and labour. With the help of macroeconomic indicators one can understand the share of the total national income that each factor of production receives.

8. Fiscal policies:

The scope of macroeconomics covers the concept of fiscal policies and the various fiscal policy instruments that are used in stabilising the economy. Fiscal policy is the means by which a government adjusts its spending levels and tax rates to monitor and influence a nation's economy. Macroeconomic analysis helps nations to decide their fiscal policies. The fiscal policies are like a guiding force that helps the government is to decide how much money to spend to support specific economic activities. It also helps them to understand how much revenue it must earn from the system to maintain economic stability.

9. Monetary policies

Monetary policies refer to the central bank activities that are directed towards influencing the quantity of money and credit in a particular economy. They are different from fiscal policies as fiscal policies are concerned with the decision of the government regarding taxation and spending. Monetary and fiscal policies are useful tools that are used for regulating economic activities in the country. The scope of macroeconomics includes both monetary and fiscal policies in order to confirm that economic activities are under control. In India, the reserve Bank of India implements the monetary policy through open market operations, bank rate policy, reserve systems, credit control policies, moral persuasion and through many other instruments. The RBI can do this only after analysing the various macroeconomic factors.

10. Policies related to balance of payments:

The scope of macroeconomics also extends to the concept of balance of payments. If there is a deficit and balance of payments it means that a country imports more capital, goods and services than it exports. A surplus and the balance of payment mean that the country's exports are more than its imports. A country's balance of payments and its net international investment position together constitute its international accounts. The macroeconomic analysis of balance of payments and international investment position are critical in deciding the national and international economic policies.

To conclude, it can be said that the scope of macroeconomics is extremely wide. The major scope of macroeconomic policies is directed towards contributing to economic and social well-being in an equitable and sustainable manner. The scope of macroeconomics also proves that the study of macroeconomics is inevitable if one has to understand how a nation prospers in the long run.

1.5. Importance of Macroeconomics:

1. **Macroeconomics is a field that is of paramount importance to almost any entity that is involved in trade and commerce.** Its principles allow the government to predict a number of things related to economic markets and monetary policies.

2. **Macroeconomics examines the determination and interaction among various aggregate variables.** It studies the causes of fluctuation in such variables and is of practical importance as far as formulation of macroeconomic policies is concerned. There are several reasons why the study of macroeconomics is important. The reasons have been listed as follows:

3. **It helps in the understanding of how the economy functions:** Macroeconomic analysis helps us to understand the functioning of a complicated macroeconomic system. It elaborates how a particular economy functions and how the level of national income and employment are determined on the basis of aggregate demand and aggregate supply.

4. **Economic growth:** macroeconomic analysis helps to achieve the goal of economic growth, higher GDP level and the higher level of employment. It helps to analyse the forces which determine economic growth of the particular economy and elaborates how to reach the highest rate of economic growth that is sustainable in the long run.

5. **Solving economic problems:** the study of macroeconomics helps to understand the various economic problems that the country faces. Problems like unemployment, poverty, deflation, inflation, stagflation etc. can be

identified and efforts can be taken to solve these problems at the macro level. Such problems cannot be solved at the micro level and the study of macroeconomics is inevitable if such problems are to be dealt with.

6. **Formulation of monetary policies:** governments and economists frequently use macroeconomic theories and principles to study the growth of the GDP of a particular nation. When monitoring policies are formulated, they must serve as a means for reducing the rates of unemployment and poverty.

7. **Predicting economic growth and stagnation:** the government uses macroeconomic analysis to prevent calamities and encourage growth in the free market. A particular government may take the decision of increasing the interest rates as a means of encouraging the customers spend lesser. Overall, macroeconomic analysis helps the government and other institutions to be prepared for the conditions of economic instability.

8. **Importance of macroeconomics for individuals and firms:** Various organisations and businesses also study macroeconomic trends with the objective of using the results as a guide towards formulating independent business policies. For example, an increase in the consumption of goods can be a result of increased consumer confidence, which could impact the decision of a company to increase its rate of production. Similarly, if a particular individual feels that there will be a recession in the next year, he will spend less and save more so that he can survive by maintaining a buffer of funds during the periods of recession. Therefore, macroeconomic analysis also helps for making decisions at the micro level.

9. **Analysing trade cycles:** macroeconomic analysis includes the analysis of trade cycles. It helps firms and businesses to be prepared for adverse situations or any kind of financial crisis.

10. **It facilitates the general welfare of people:** the study of macroeconomics gives a broader perspective of various social issues at the national level. In India it is observed that the population is growing fast but the economy is not growing at the same rate. This has caused unemployment and has attracted a number of social evils. Macroeconomics helps us to understand the reasons behind rising inequality and what can be done to combat it.

11. **Evaluating the effectiveness of the government:** Macroeconomic analysis observes the relationship between the economy and monetary and fiscal policy. The monetary and fiscal policies are decided by the government.

Macroeconomic analysis helps us to know the overall impact and effectiveness of the policies.

12. **Balance of payments:** The study of macroeconomics explains the factors which determine the balance of payments. It helps in identifying the causes of deficit and balance of payments and also suggests measures that should be undertaken to correct the situation.

1.6. Limitations of macroeconomics:

1. **It ignores the individual:** The study of macroeconomics ignores the actions of individual firms, consumers, producers et cetera. It lays very less focus on the welfare of individual firms or individual consumers. It is concerned with the study of aggregates and studies the impact of various factors at the macro level.

2. **False generalisations:** the logic and conclusions which may be true for individuals or small units tend to be false if applied to the whole system. There are several generalisations that have been derived from individuals and applied to the whole system. This can be misleading, irrelevant and dangerous. What is true at the macro level need not be too at the micro level.

3. **Wrong predictions:** various policies that are framed on the basis of the whole economy sometimes may be hazardous for some forms and commodities. For example, if the general price level appears to be fixed it does not mean that the prices of all the commodities are stable and unchanged. This is because the price of some commodities can decrease while the prices of other commodities can increase and cause an adjustment effect that leads to the same general price level. Such macroeconomic indicators do not give the true position of things.

4. **The problems related to aggregate of approach:** the study of macroeconomics is obsessed with their creative approach. Excessive thinking in terms of lumping the individual units together may lead to wrong inferences. Individual units possess exclusive traits and are not homogeneous. Here are a few examples which would make the meaning of the above statement clear:

   a. Food versus Apples
   b. Money supply versus paper currency
   c. General unemployment rate versus the unemployment rate of teachers

In each of the above examples it can be seen that macroeconomics always studies food, money supply or general unemployment rate as a single variable. As a matter of fact, this approach is wrong as it leads to wrong inferences.

5. **The general unemployment rate is a macroeconomic variable.** For a particular country or general unemployment rate may be very low but the unemployment rate of teachers may be very high. Therefore, having a favourable employment rate does not mean that all the people are equally employed. The tendency to aggregate everything does not influence all the sectors of the economy in the same manner. The general rise in prices for example may not affect all the sectors of the economy in the similar manner. There may be some sections that have been affected adversely as compared to others.

6. **Difficulties in measurement:** The entire macroeconomic analysis cannot be very precise as the different elements that constitute an aggregate are of a heterogeneous nature. While measuring the aggregates everything is measured in terms of money. For example, the aggregate consumption, income, saving and investment are all measured in terms of money and not in terms of goods or services which are of heterogeneous nature. However, the value of money itself is not stable which makes it difficult to make meaningful comparisons of economic aggregates over a period of time.

7. **Macroeconomic paradoxes:** There are several paradoxes in macroeconomics. For example, a particular firm can achieve higher profits by reducing the wages paid to the workers. However, if all the firms attempt to do the same, total consumption will fall at the macro level and will affect the sales and profits. In another example, at the micro level saving is a good habit. However, if the majority of the population start saving and not spending at all, the overall consumption will fall and will reduce the output. The economy may shrink and cause adverse situations and lead to a fall in actual saving. Therefore, what is true at the micro level is not always true at the macro level and vice versa.

8. **The wrong use of macroeconomic policies can lead to disasters.** For example, the Indian government announced demonetisation in the year 2016. We all are experiencing the ill effects of demonetisation. It was also implemented wrongly, and several people lost their lives. It requires skill, knowledge, maturity and expertise to frame and implement macroeconomic policies.

1.7. Difference between Microeconomics and Macroeconomics

1. Meaning:

Microeconomics deals with the analysis of individual economic units. It is a study of particular markets, and segments of the economy. It studies consumer behaviour, individual labour markets and the theory of firms.

Macroeconomic studies the entire nation's economy as a whole and considers various aggregates like national output and inflation rates for the purpose of macroeconomic analysis.

2. Areas of concern:

Microeconomics is concerned with the income, output, and performance of individual firms or prices of individual goods.

Macroeconomics is a study of aggregates such as national income, national output and studies general price levels.

3. Equilibrium:

Microeconomics helps in order to understand how equilibrium can be achieved at a small scale.

Macroeconomics on the other hand, determines the equilibrium levels of employment and income of the entire country or a particular economy.

4. Focus:

The major focus of macroeconomics is on overcoming the issues concerning the allocation of scarce resources.

Macroeconomics focuses on issues like rate of unemployment, poverty, per capita national income et cetera.

5. Demand and supply:

Microeconomics account for the factors like demand and supply for a specific good or service in a particular market.

Macroeconomics deals with aggregate demand an aggregate supply for a particular nation. It studies the productive capacity of an entire economy.

6. Approach:

Microeconomics is concerned with the supply and demand and other forces that determine the price level is in the economy. It takes a bottom-up approach to analyse the economy. It tries to understand the choices that human beings make, there are decisions and the way they allocate resources.

Macroeconomics studies the behaviour of the entire nation and how the policies impact the economy as a whole. It analyses the industries and economies as against individuals are specific forms and follows a top-down approach.

7. Usefulness:

Macroeconomics analysis is useful in regulating the prices of a product alongside the prices of factors of production like land, labour, entrepreneur, capital. Macroeconomic analysis on the other hand, deals with the broad price levels and attempts to achieve a control over the evils of deflation, inflation, stagflation, poverty, unemployment and the overall welfare of the people in a particular country.

8. Internal versus external environment:

Microeconomics is more concerned with the internal environment of a business. Macroeconomics on the other hand, is concerned with the external environment of business.

9. Behaviour of the investors:

As far as the behaviour of investors is concerned, microeconomics plays a more important role as compared to macroeconomics according to some experts. For example, John Templeton was a successful value investor once said "I never asked of the market is going to go up or down because I don't know. It doesn't matter. I search nation after nation for stocks asking: 'there is the one that is lowest price in relation to what I believe its worth?'

10. Some similarities:

Overall, though there are several differences between microeconomics, they also share some similarities. Factors that may directly affect microeconomic environments can also have an impact on macroeconomic factors in the long run. Similarly, when the government deploys policies at the national level of the state-level, it affects the individual consumers and businesses. For example, introduction of GST created several problems and confusions among the trading class in India. It also deeply affected the consumer buying behaviour at the individual level.

According to Adam Smith in his book "The Wealth of Nations", microeconomic and macroeconomic factors both share the same focus- the allocation of scarce resources. Both branches of economics study how the demand for a certain resource interacts with the ability to supply that particular good. They both determine how to best distribute and allocate the scarce resources among several end-users. Microeconomics and macroeconomics, both deal with maximisation. While microeconomics deals with profit maximisation perform and deals with concepts like consumer surplus, macroeconomics deals with the maximisation of national income and growth.

1.8. Objectives of Macroeconomic:

The primary objective of macroeconomic policies is to maximise national income and bring about economic growth and development to the nation. Macroeconomics aims at raising the levels of utilities and the standard of living of the entire economy and its components. There are several secondary macroeconomic objectives. They have been listed as follows:

1. Sustainable growth and development:

In the year 1997, Alassane D. Ouattara, the Deputy Managing Director of the International Monetary Fund defined sustainable economic growth as "economic growth that brings lasting employment gains and poverty reduction; provides greater equality of income through greater equality of opportunity, including for women; and protects the environment." The third element, "protects the environment" Therefore, one of the major macroeconomic objectives of a nation is to bring about economic growth and development that has a long-lasting positive impact and leads to poverty reduction. Macroeconomic policies also aim at protecting the environment and providing equality of income without sacrificing the element of 'equal opportunities to all'.

According to 2017 figures, China accounts for almost 30% of the world's Fossil CO_2 Emission. This is certainly not an example of sustainable economic development. Clearly, the macroeconomic policies of the "bat soup country" are unethical, immoral, coercive, dictatorial and non-sustainable in nature. It is known to us how China was horrendously irresponsible in controlling the spread of the novel corona virus which caused chaos and mayhem, making the year 2020 the worst year of the decade for the whole world. The economies which aim at development in the non-sustainable, immoral and unethical manner fail in the long run and prove to be disastrous to the entire world. Therefore, it must be noted that though the primary objective of macroeconomics is to bring about national growth and development, it is important that such development must be sustainable and ethical in nature.

2. Achieving full employment:

Full employment is a situation in which all the available labour resources are being used in the most efficient way as possible. When there is full employment, the highest amount of skilled and unskilled labour is employed in a given economy at any given point of time. The concept of full employment is actually theoretical and impractical. Therefore, economists define various types of full employment based on their theories for deciding the goals of macroeconomic policies. Therefore, it can be said that full employment involves zero or very low unemployment rates. The major objective of macroeconomics is to bring about full employment and reduce the social and economic costs of high unemployment. If there is high unemployment, there will be lesser consumption which will then lead to more poverty. If the rate of employment is low, naturally people will earn less and pay less tax. This will also affect the government revenues. It will force the government to borrow funds from other financial institutions and create a separate platter of problems. Unemployment is actually very undesirable also because it leads to increased crime rates, social alienation, vandalism and a feeling of discontent and depression among qualified candidates who are not having any jobs. Therefore, the macroeconomic objective of achieving full employment is extremely important for the overall success of an economy.

3. Price stability:

Price stability is one of the most critical goals of macroeconomics. The monetary and fiscal policies are aimed to support sustainable rates of economic activities. Governments try to design their macroeconomic policies to maintain a very low rate of inflation or deflation. Inflation is a rise in the general price levels of goods and services that result in a decline of the value of money and the overall purchasing power. Deflation on the other hand, is a decrease in the general price level of goods or services over a longer period of time. Deflation threatens economic growth as in situations of deflation, the general price level declines and people postpone consumption and companies postpone investments. Rapid inflation is also very dangerous as it makes economic decision-making more complicated and slows economic growth due to the reduced purchasing power of people. Usually, a low rate of inflation of around 2% helps investors and spenders plan their investments and spending properly. The ideal target of 2% is useful for countries to stay away from deflation or higher levels of inflation that leads to an economic downfall. Therefore, macroeconomic analysis aims at bringing about price stability which contributes to achieving high levels of economic activity and employment.

4. Equilibrium in balance of payments:

The balance of payments is a record of all of the transactions that take place between the citizens of one nation and the residents of all of the other nations in the globe during the course of a specific time period. This time frame is typically capped at one year in the vast majority of instances. On the other hand, the monthly calculation of the balance of payments is utilised by several nations. The primary goal of macroeconomics is to devise policies that will result in the balance of payments being in a state of equilibrium. To maintain an open economy without persistently high levels of unemployment requires a condition of the balance of payments known as equilibrium, which exists for a specific length of time and allows for the possibility of doing so. A state of equilibrium can be said to occur when both a country's exports and imports are in the correct proportions to one another. It is not ideal for an economy to have a significant imbalance in its balance of payments, either in the form of a deficit or a surplus. A country that maintains a stable equilibrium in its balance of payments is better able to bring in foreign cash and offer a wider variety of goods and services to its domestic market, both of which are beneficial to consumers. India, like the vast majority of other countries, has consistently been dealing with a significant imbalance in its balance of payments. This is due to the fact that in order for India's economy to function normally, it requires increased levels of foreign money, technology, and other resources. As a result of this circumstance, there is a deficit in the balance of payments since the payments that our nation has paid are higher than the payments that the government has received. A significant trade deficit is a reflection of an imbalanced economy in which there is a high demand from consumers but the industrial sector is weak and unable to fulfil the present demand from consumers because of the trade deficit.

The current account and the capital account together make up the balance of payment account. The current account comes first, followed by the capital account. The current account is concerned with the flow of money that is generated as a result of the money that is earned and spent as a result of the trade in goods and services. The capital account is concerned with all of the transactions that take place within the nation that pertain to assets such as land, foreign currency, bank deposits, and so on and so forth.

This information is current as of January-March 2020 and was published on July 1, 2020. When compared to the deficit of USD 4.7 billion that was established in the Jan-Mar quarter of 2019 and the surplus of USD 2.6 billion that was posted in the preceding quarter, India's current account balance posted a marginal surplus of USD 0.6 billion (0.1% of GDP) in the Jan-Mar quarter of 2020.

A current account deficit will occur in a country when the domestic currency is overvalued, there is growth in the economy, and there is also an element of diminishing competitiveness in the economy. It is necessary for there to be a surplus in the capital account so that the current account deficit may be balanced out. A surplus in the current accounts can sometimes cancel out a shortfall in the capital accounts, which can happen when those accounts are out of balance. The government needs to come up with macroeconomic policies that would dissuade people from purchasing things that are imported from other countries. Keynesian economists promote the strategy known as "expenditure switching," in which the majority of the items that are imported are replaced with those that are manufactured locally. The macroeconomic policies of the government are geared at encouraging domestic production as a means of displacing the commodities and services that are imported as part of this effort. In order for the government to control the amount of goods that may be imported, they impose taxes, quotas, and embargoes. Depreciation of the currency is another strategy that governments use to reduce the current account deficit. When a currency appreciates, imports become more expensive at the macroeconomic level; thus, this has an effect on a country's marginal willingness to bring in goods from other countries. As a result of the decline in the value of the currency, exports also become cheaper to foreign buyers. As a direct consequence of this, the nation is able to export more goods, which has a beneficial effect on the overall balance of payments. Because of this, the overarching goal of macroeconomic policy is to ensure that there is a healthy equilibrium between a nation's imports and exports over the course of time.

5. **Equitable distribution of income and wealth:**

Macroeconomic policies aim for equal distribution of income and wealth. When income and wealth is equally distributed it shows the signs of a well-to-do economy where everyone has equal opportunities, income and wealth. When there is equitable distribution of income and wealth, no sections of the economy are better off than the other and the income gap is not too wide.

6. **Social objectives:**

A special branch of economics called social macroeconomics studies the role of social integration and social fragmentation in shaping the macroeconomic performance of a nation. Effective implementation of macroeconomic policies requires social cooperation which cannot be ignored. One of the major macroeconomic objectives is to achieve the social cooperation by making sure that the needs of the society are met at the macroeconomic level. Macroeconomic policies aim to achieve the objective of 'fair or equitable distribution of income' due to which the gap between the rich and the poor is not too large. In a study performed in the United States of America in the year 1990 suggested that loss of life from income equality in the United States was equivalent to the combined loss of life due to lung cancer, diabetes, motor vehicle accidents, HIV-related causes, suicide and homicide. Therefore, macroeconomic policies should aim at social welfare by implementing measures at the macroeconomic level. Studies have also shown that there is a correlation between income inequality and health and social problems. Therefore, the macroeconomic objective of social welfare has its own significance in economic development.

7. Productivity

Productivity is a measure of the efficiency with which a particular country combines the forces of labour and capital to produce more with the same level of factor inputs. Productivity determines the overall standard of living and also gives an idea of how a particular country uses its resources to produce a given output. It is popularly said that "productivity isn't everything, but in the long run it's almost everything". The macroeconomic objective of increasing the productivity leads to higher profits, wages and supports economic growth. Due to higher productivity, the cost of the goods that are sold to the consumers also reduces and the consumers can enjoy the advantage of buying high-quality products at a lower cost. It encourages domestic producers to sell standardised goods and services at competitive prices. This enables the consumers to buy goods that have been produced by domestic manufacturers instead of goods that have been imported. Due to higher wages, the overall consumption increases and also generates more tax revenue for the government. Overall, it can be said that the macroeconomic objective of achieving productivity is of paramount importance.

1.9. Questions

1. What are the differences between microeconomics and macroeconomics?
2. Explain the meaning of macroeconomics and its scope.
3. Explain the importance and objectives of macroeconomics.
4. Explain the importance and limitations of macroeconomics.
5. What is the meaning of macroeconomics? Explain the nature of macroeconomics.

Chapter 2

National Income

2.1. Meaning:

National income refers to the values of the goods and services provided by the country during the financial year. It is the net result of all the economic activities of a particular country during a period of time-usually one year. National income is valued in monetary terms. The measurement of national income is significant as it helps us to understand the overall size of the economy and the level of country's economic performance. Calculating national income makes it easy to compare the standard of living of people from different nations. With the help of the statistics related to national income, a particular country can trace the trend or speed of economic growth in relation to previous years. Therefore, it can be said that national income is one of the most crucial concepts in macroeconomic analysis. To gain a better understanding about national income, let us study some definitions in the next section.

National income is an aggregate value of total income earned by all individuals, businesses, and organizations within a country's borders during a specific period. It consists total income generated from various sources, such as wages and salaries, profits, rental income, interest, and dividends.

The national income reflects the economic health of a country. It helps to policymakers in decision-making process regarding taxation, government spending, and other economic policies. National income is measured through the gross domestic product (GDP). It is a total value of all goods and services produced within a country's borders during a specific period.

National Income would be measured through Gross National Income (GNI), Net National Income (NNI) and per capita income. GNI is the aggregate total of Income generated by a country's residents and it's also including income generated from abroad. NNI is the calculating by deducting depreciation of capital assets from GNI. Per capita income is the average total of Income of each, and every person of a country and it's calculated by dividing the total national income by total population of the Nation.

2.2. Definitions of National Income:

According to Alfred Marshall, "The labour and capital of country acting on its natural resources produce annually a certain net aggregate of commodities, material and immaterial including services of all kinds. This is the true net annual income or revenue of the country or national dividend."

Marshall's definition of national income is theoretically sound, simple and comprehensive. However, the definition given by Alfred Marshall has some practical limitations. It is impossible to make a perfect estimate of the total production of goods and services in a particular country. There can be problems such as double counting. Similarly, the portion of the produce that is retained for personal consumption can remain unaccounted for. Therefore, the definition is not perfect and gives a vague idea of what national income is.

According to the National income committee of India, 1951," a national income estimate measures the volume of commodities and services turned out during a given period counted without duplication.

The definition given by the National income committee of India mentioned that it is an estimate. According to the committee, it measures the volume of commodities and services turned out and avoid duplication. Therefore, the definition clearly states that the limitation of duplication is avoided while calculating the national income.

According to A.C. Pigou, "National income is that part of objective income of the community, including of course income derived from abroad which can be measured in terms of money."

The definition given by A.C.Pigou is convenient, flexible, precise and practical as it does not require measuring the national income in a way Alfred Marshall insisted. The definition given by A.C.Pigou makes an artificial distinction between goods and that in exchange for money and goods that are not so exchanged. Unfortunately, the total amount of national dividend cannot be correctly derived according to A.C.Pigou's definition because one is expected to include only those goods and services that can be exchanged for money. In cases where there is barter exchange, A.C.Pigou's definition is of no use.

According to Fisher, "The national income or national dividend consists solely of services as serviced by ultimate consumers, whether from their materials or from the human environments. Thus, a piano, or an overcoat made for me this year is not a part of this year's income, but in addition to the capital. Only the services rendered to me this year by these things are income."

According to Fisher, the concept of national income can be measured with the help of measuring consumption. According to Fisher the national income for a particular country is determined by its annual consumption. Fisher's definition is more welfare oriented as it considers the consumption of goods and services that are made available to the people in the country. If the people in a particular country have the privilege of consuming certain goods and services, it certainly affects their standard of living and overall welfare. Unfortunately, it is very difficult to get an idea of net consumption as compared to net production. If a particular commodity or good lasts beyond one year, it is very difficult to quantify the consumption of such goods. Therefore, again the definition fails to give a perfect idea about the national income of a particular country.

According to Simon Kuznets, "National income is the net output of commodities and services flowing during the year from the country's productive system in the hands of the ultimate consumers."

According to Hicks, "National income is a collection of goods and services reduced to a common basis by being measured in terms of money."

According to Prof. Samuelson, "It is the loose name we give for the money measure of the overall annual flow of goods and services in an economy."

Prof. Ackley defines national income as the sum of all:

(a) Wages, salaries, commissions, bonuses, and other forms of employee earnings.

(b) Net income from rentals and royalties.

(c) Interest income, and

(d) Profits.

Therefore, several authors have made an attempt to define national income. The above-mentioned definitions suggest that national income is the net and final value of all the products and services of a particular economy during a particular time period. The above definitions also tell us that the national income is counted in terms of money and duplication should be avoided while calculating national income. National income can be measured according to some authors with the help of the value of goods and services produced. Fisher on the other hand, propagates that national income must be measured in terms of consumption rather than production. The definitions also give us an idea that the net gains from international transactions are also included in the national income.

2.3. Concepts of National Income.

2.3.1. Gross National product (GNP)

Gross National product or GNP is the total value of all finished goods and services produced by a country's citizens in a given financial year, irrespective of their location. This means that Gross National product also includes the total value of all finished goods and services produced by the citizens of a country who are not living in that country currently. GNP considers the investments made by the businesses and residents of the country who are living both inside and in foreign countries. It also considers the value of the products that are manufactured by the industries of domestic origin. GNP is an important indicator and helps in fighting the evils of poverty and inflation.

There are three different approaches for the purpose of calculating the gross national product:

A. Expenditure approach.

B. Income approach.

C. Value-added approach.

A. Expenditure approach.

For the purpose of determining the gross national product, all of the money spent on personal consumption, money spent by the government, money invested in the private sector of the economy, money made through net exports, and money acquired from other nations are put together. A deduction is made from the income received by non-native residents inside the economy. After deducting the value of a nation's imports from the value of its exports, one arrives at the value of net exports for that country.

Under the expenditure approach, GNP is the addition of the following factors:

1. Investments.

2. Government expenditure.

3. Consumption expenditure.

4. Net exports (arrived by deducting imports from total exports).

5. Net income (arrived by deducting the income earned by foreigners in the country from income earned by the residents in foreign countries)

The mathematical formula for calculating GNP according to the expenditure approach is as follows:

Y = C+I+G+X+Z

Where Y means GNP,

C means consumption expenditure,

G is for government expenditure

X is for net exports and

Z is for net income.

Alternatively, the gross national product can be also calculated as follows:

GNP = GDP + net income inflow from overseas - net income outflow to foreign countries.

Where GDP is the gross domestic product which is equal to the addition of investments, consumption, government expenditure and net exports (arrive by deducting the imports from the exports)

For the purpose of calculating gross national product, one must take into account the manufacture of tangible goods such as plants, equipment, machinery, vehicles. One should also consider the value of services like professional consultancy, healthcare, education, hospitality services et cetera. The concept of GNP also includes access and appreciation. It must be noted that the cost of services that are used in producing the goods should not be computed independently as it will be included in the cost of finished products. For example, if a particular car is polished by the manufacturer, before being sold to the final consumer, the cost of publishing services must not be considered separately as it forms the part of the final good.

The income of the foreign nationals is not taken into account while calculating the gross national product. If a foreign company has manufacturing units in the country, the total output of such foreign companies is also not considered for the purpose of calculating GNP.

B. Income approach:

Under the income approach, GNP is calculated by measuring the income earnings received by the country's factors of production mainly-land, labour and capital.

The mathematical formula for calculating GNP according to the income approach is as follows.

GNP= Wages+ Interest income + Rental Income + Profit + dividends + undistributed profits + depreciation + direct and indirect taxes + net income from abroad.

In the above formula, wages represent the salaries, earnings or income of the residents during the entire year. Interest income represents any income earned in the form of interest from bank savings accounts, treasury bills or interest earned on foreign investments. Rental income includes any income that is earned from renting and owned property. It includes the income that people learn by renting houses, office spaces, rooms or apartments. GNP also includes undistributed profits and profits distributed by the way of dividend to the shareholders. It also considers depreciation on assets and direct/indirect taxes. Net income from abroad is derived by deducting the imports from the total exports.

C. Value-added approach in calculating the GNP:

According to the value-added approach to GNP, the money value of final goods and services produced at current prices during a particular year is considered. This avoids double counting.

For the purpose of calculating gross national product, only the final services and goods are taken into consideration. Intermediate goods are avoided. The reason behind avoiding intermediate goods is that these goods are bought for further processing or resale and of such goods are considered for the purpose of calculating the GNP, it would lead to a case of double counting and give a wrong idea. For example, if a particular dairy sells milk worth ₹ 1000 to a sweet manufacturer, who converts that milk into sweets and sells it for ₹ 1500 to the final consumer, the value of milk and the value of sweets will get added up twice as the sweets have been derived out of the same milk. Final goods and services referred to those goods which are used either for consumption or for the purpose of investment. For example, goods purchased by the consumer households, goods purchased by the firms for capital formation or investment like machines, plants, tools et cetera are examples of final goods. The final goods are not purchased for further processing and resale. On the other hand, intermediate goods referred to those goods which are used either for resale or for further production in the same year. For example, milk is purchased by a dairy shop or milk used for making chocolates. Intermediate goods are usually purchased by a particular manufacturing unit from some other supplier who manufactures it. When goods are meant for resale, they should be treated as intermediate goods.

At each stage of production, value gets added to a particular product. For example, if a cloth manufacturer sells cloth to garment manufacturer with rupees hundred, the garment manufacturer would convert that cloth into a shirt and sell it to the wholesaler for ₹ 350. Here, ₹ 250 is the value-added to the original cloth. If the same process is carried out and all such differences are added up for all the industries in a particular economy, we arrive at the value of the gross national product using the value-added approach.

The mathematical formula for calculating gross national product according to the value-added approach is as follows:

GNP (value-added approach) = Gross value added + Net income from abroad.

2.3.2. Gross National Product at market prices

Gross National product in the market price is defined as the market value of all the final goods and services that are produced within a particular country by the residents during a particular era and also includes net factor income from abroad.

Since we consider the market value of all the final goods and services, depreciation and indirect taxes also need to be included.

However, the following things are not supposed to be included in the calculation of GNP:

1. Transactions that are purely of financial nature - buying and selling of shares bonds and securities.

Transfer payments made by the government.

Private transfers.

2. Transfer of goods that have been used or second-hand goods.

3. Barter transactions and transactions that cannot be measured in terms of money.

4. Income from illegal activities like smuggling, drug trafficking, contract killing, sale of illegal arms, gambling et cetera.

5. Other things that cannot be counted in terms of money for example services of a housewife or plumbing faults repaired by the house owner himself.

2.3.3. Gross National Product at factor costs:

There are several factors of production including land, plant and machinery, labour and capital. These factors produce income on a continual basis. When the income of all such factors as added, it amounts to Gross National product at factor costs. The calculation of GNP at factor cost includes depreciation but excludes the indirect taxes. Therefore, indirect taxes have to be deducted from the GNP at market prices in order to arrive at a GNP at factor cost. The government provides subsidies for the purpose of the use of various factors of production. Therefore, subsidies must be included in the calculation of the gross national product factor costs. Therefore, the mathematical formula for calculating GNP at factor cost is as follows:

GNP at factor cost = GNP at market prices -Indirect taxes + Government subsidies.

2.3.4. Net National Product:

Net national product is calculated by deducting the depreciation from the gross national product. As compared to the gross national product, net national product is a more accurate measure of the total value of the goods and services produced by a country in a particular year. It is an indicator of the total productivity of a particular country. The mathematical formula for net national product is as follows:

NNP = GNP - Depreciation.

Economists use the net national product as a tool to report the growth and strength of a nation and can be used to evaluate a particular country's growth as compared to other countries. It also reflects the health of the markets in a particular country.

2.3.5. Net national product at market prices:

When depreciation is deducted from the gross national product at market prices, the net national product at market prices is derived. However, when we talk about market prices, it must be noted that market prices include the indirect taxes that are imposed by the government.

2.3.6. Net National Product factor costs:

Net national product at factor cost is also referred to as national income. It is the sum total of value-added at factor cost or net domestic product at factor cost and net factor income earned from abroad. It is derived by deducting the net indirect taxes from the net national product at market prices.

When the Net National product is calculated at market prices, it includes subsidies and indirect taxes. When indirect taxes are levied, it increases the value of the product of the service. Therefore, the indirect taxes must be subtracted in order to calculate net national product at factor costs. Similarly, subsidies reduce the value of the product or service. Therefore, subsidies must be added to calculate the true value of the net national product at factor costs.

For example, that is assumed that a manufacturer produces a particular product and the cost of production including profit of the manufacturer is hundred rupees. For producing that particular product, the manufacturer has to make use of different factors of production such as land, labour and capital. If the government subsidises the production of this product at ₹ 5, and also imposes taxes to the amount of ₹ 25, the net market price of the product will be: *100 (cost of production plus profit) +25(taxes levied by the government) -5 (government subsidy) = 120.*

When such a goods sold, the manufacturer would get a total sum of ₹ 105, which would be distributed among various factors of production. Therefore, if one wants to arrive to the factor costs to the figures of market costs, the factor cost will be equal to the market cost minus indirect taxes plus the subsidies. In the case of our example, it will be 120-125+5=100. It must be noted that NNP at factor costs does not include depreciation.

Therefore, the mathematical formula for NNP at factor cost is as follows:

NNP at factor cost = NNP at market price - Net indirect taxes + subsidy.

OR

NNP at factor cost = GNP at market price - Depreciation- Net indirect taxes + subsidy.

2.3.7. Gross Domestic Product:

The gross domestic product is the sum total of the market value of the final goods and services produced within a particular country during the financial year including the depreciation. If depreciation is subtracted from the GDP, we get the net domestic product. GDP counts all the output generated by a particular country within its domestic borders.

Gross domestic product = Consumption + Investment + Government purchases + Exports - Imports.

Therefore, the gross domestic product includes the following components:

1. Direct Taxes.

2. Wages (including salaries)

3. Rent and Interest

4. Dividends and undistributed profits.

5. Mixed income*

(*According to The Organisation for Economic Co-operation and Development (OECD) "Mixed income is the surplus or deficit accruing from production by unincorporated enterprises owned by households; it implicitly contains an element of remuneration for work done by the owner, or other members of the household, that cannot be separately identified from the return to the owner as entrepreneur, but it excludes the operating surplus coming from owner-occupied dwelling.")

For the purpose of calculating GDP a particular product has to be actually produced for the purpose of consumption. GDP cannot include intermediate goods that are used for producing something else. At the same time, GDP includes only those products and services that are produced within the domestic borders of the country.

To sum up, GDP does not include the following:

1. Unpaid work (work done at home or by volunteers): this means that if a particular baker bakes a loaf of bread for a customer, it would be included in the GDP. But if he bakes the same loaf to be consumed for his family, it will not be included in the GDP.

2. Illegal goods or services (black market).

3. Transfer payments made by the government.

4. Goods and services that are not produced domestically are not included in calculating GDP.

The gross domestic product of a country is a widely used term to express the health of national and global economies. A growth in GDP (without a problematic level of inflation) reflects the overall prosperity of the working class and the businessmen of a country.

GDP in India is expected to reach 2610.00 USD Billion by the end of the year 2020. It is expected to trend around 2850 billion US dollars in the year 2021 and around 3000 USD billion dollars in the year 2022 according to predictions based on reliable models.

Theoretically, GDP can be studied using three different approaches:

A. The production approach: according to the production approach, the value-added at each stage of production is summed up. Here, value-added refers to the total sales less the value of intermediate inputs into the production process. For example, cloth would be an intermediate input and a T-shirt would be the final product. Or a civil engineer's services would be an intermediate input and a flyover would be the final product.

B. The expenditure approach: according to the expenditure approach, the value of purchases made by the final consumers is added up. For example, people by food products, computers or avail medical services. It also includes investments made by companies in machineries and the purchase of goods and services by the government and foreigners.

C. The income approach. According to this approach, the total income generated by productive activities is summed up. It includes the wages or compensation that the workers and employees receive and also the surplus or profits of the companies.

In the year 2015, our country changed its method of calculating the GDP by making some dramatic revisions. For example, before the year 2015 the formula for calculating GDP was as follows:

GDP = Private Consumption + Gross Investment + Government Investment + Government Spending + (Exports- Imports)

However, in the year 2015, the Central statistics office adopted an international practice of GDP at market prices and the gross value addition measure to estimate economic activity. Therefore, from the year 2015 GDP at market price was considered as follows:

GDP at market price = GDP at factor cost + Indirect Taxes − Subsidies.

The base year for calculating GDP was also updated. As a result, the economy grew by 6.9% in the year. Using the previous methodology, GDP expansion in that year was 4.7%. However, Unemployment rate in India shot up to a five-year high of 5 per cent in 2015-16. The point to be noted here is that though GDP is one of the most important indicators of economic performance, it is not entirely reliable and fails to give the true picture. The following section would discuss the limitations of GDP as an economic indicator:

Limitations of GDP as an economic indicator:

1. It does not consider the underground economy or the black market. In some countries, the scale of underground economies is huge.

2. In many developing countries, there is very less consideration given to the environmental issues. Such environmental damage caused by developing countries that rely on higher output to support economic growth should be actually counted against the country's GDP. The current methods of calculating GDP do not consider the environmental damage caused by these countries.

3. The concept of GDP fails to consider the quality aspect of production. For example, several smart phone manufacturers are continually updating their line of products with better displays and advanced processors. This is enabling the consumers to enjoy more quality and utility at the same cost. Such advancements are not counted in GDP as it is very difficult to quantify the relative utility generated.

4. Goods that are produced for private consumption are not recorded officially. Farmers who produce at the level of subsistence (limited to own use) are completely ignored in the GDP calculations.

5. There is a huge impact of political pressure on the methods of calculating GDP. Cunning politicians can make continuous attempts to alter the data and the methods of calculating GDP to paint a rosy picture that does not actually exist.

6. An ideal indicator of a particular nation's performance must include both income and non-income variables such as literacy rates, employment rates, life expectancy, measures of inequality et cetera. A higher GDP does not mean that the people of a particular nation are living better quality of life.

7. In case of countries where a considerable percentage of the workforce is employed in informal sectors (such as 'frying pakodas in the street'), their incomes may not be considered for the purpose of calculating the nation's GDP.

2.3.8. Private Income:

According to the Central statistics organisation, "private income is the total of factor incomes from all sources and current transfers from the government and the rest of the world accruing to the private sector". Therefore, private income includes the national income; transfer payments interest on public debts, Social Security but excludes profits and surplus of public enterprises. Therefore, the mathematical formula for calculating private income is as follows:

Private income = National Income + Transfer Payments + Social Security+ Interest in Public Debts - Profits and Surplus of Public Enterprises.

2.3.9. Personal Income:

Prof. W.C. Peterson defines Personal Income as "the income actually received by persons from all sources in the form of current transfer payments and factor income". Personal income is thus the total income that is earned by the individuals of a country in a particular area from all sources before direct taxes.

The mathematical formula for calculating personal income is as follows:

Personal income = Private income + undistributed profits - direct taxes

2.3.10. Disposable income:

A person's "disposable income" is "the income remaining with individuals after deduction of all taxes levied against the income and their property by the government," as defined by Professor WC Peterson. As a result, when people talk about their "disposable income," they are referring to the revenue that really comes into their families from a variety of various sources. Because this revenue is obtained after subtracting the direct taxes (for example, revenue Tax) paid by the individual, it can be disposed of according to the individual's will even if the taxes were paid directly by the individual.

The mathematical formula for calculating disposable income is as follows:

Disposable Income = Personal Income - Direct Taxes - Miscellaneous receipts from the Government.

2.4. Circular flow of income.

As far as the study of macroeconomics is concerned, there are four macroeconomics sectors.

Household Sector - This sector consists of all the individuals and families in the. The household sector provides the various factors of production. Through the households, labour, land, capital and enterprise are some basic inputs that are provided for the purpose of production. The household sector also comprises of the individuals who consume the products and services that are manufactured by the industry. By consuming the products, they create earning opportunities for the industrial sector by paying for the purchase of products and services.

The firm's sector - This is the sector which includes all the business enterprises, partnerships, sole trading concerns, companies and other forms of business organisations. The sector primarily focuses on manufacturing of goods and provision of services that are sold in the market. While manufacturing such goods or services, the owners of these enterprises have to make payments and provide remuneration to the various factors of production. They must pay rent for the purpose of using land and also pay wages to the labour.

The government sectors - The local, state and central government are a part of this sector. The basic function of this particular sector is to regulate the functioning of the entire economy by formulating laws and stating rules that must be followed by all. The government also makes amendments in several policies that are aimed towards the development of the different sectors of the economy. The government sector charges direct and indirect taxes to individuals and enterprises and earns revenue from them. The government also spends funds for the purpose of building infrastructure and providing subsidies to certain sectors of the economy. A major part of government spending is also done for providing essential services to the public and maintain a certain level of public welfare.

The foreign sector - The foreign sector defines the transactions of the country with the rest of the world. It deals with imports and exports. One can arrive at a value of net imports by deducting the imports from the exports. Domestic goods are produced and exported to other countries. Similarly, various imports of goods and services produced abroad enable the sale of foreign goods and services to the domestic consumers.

The circular flow of income in two sector model:

Adam Smith in his book the Wealth of Nations correctly mentions that "What is annually saved is as regularly consumed as what is annually spent, and nearly at the same time too; but it is consumed by a different set of people. That portion of his revenue which a rich man annually spends is in most cases consumed by idle guests...That portion which he annually saves, as for the sake of the profit it is immediately employed as a capital, is consumed in the same manner...but by a different set of people".

The circular flow of income or the circular flow model is a model of the economy in which the major exchanges are represented as flow of services, goods and money. It is a continuous process that represents the unending flows of production of goods and services, expenditure and income is in a particular economy over a given period of time. It represents how income is distributed in the circular way between the manufacturers or service providers and the households.

John Maynard Keynes was the first economist to introduce the theories of circular flow of income in his book 'the Gen theory of employment, interest and money'. The book was published in the year 1936.

2.4.1. Circular flow of income in a two-sector model.

- By studying the circular flow of income in the two-sector model, we consider an economy which has only two sectors. Clearly, such economy cannot exist in practical circumstances. Therefore, the model is purely hypothetical in nature. The model provides a simple and convenient way to understand the Keynesian theory of income determination. The two sectors that are assumed for the purpose of studying this model are: A. Households, D. Firms. The outlays considered for the purpose of the study are only consumption and investment.

- The factors of production are owned by the households. They said factor services to earn factor incomes that are in turn spend for the consumption of the goods and services which are provided by the manufacturing firms or the service providers.

- The firm's hire the factors of production from the households at a cost. Using the services of these factors, the firms manufacture goods and provide services to the households.

Assumptions of the model:

1. No savings: One major assumption of the model is that the firms and households do not save or retain any of their earnings. In the circular flow of income, the total income earned by the households accrues and it equals to their disposable personal income which is spent on buying the goods and services provided by the industries.

2. There are only two sectors: Another significant assumption made by the model is that there are only two sectors in the economy: households and businesses.

3. The absence of international commerce: According to this concept, there are no imports or exports; alternatively, all external outflows are converted into internal inflows, and international trade does not take place at all. The model assumes that there is no external commerce of any type and that the economy is completely closed.

4. Nonexistence of the government: The model assumes that there is no government and therefore there are no direct or indirect taxes. The government does not incur any expenditure on public welfare or does not get involved into any kind of transfer payments. Even if a government exist it does not interfere or intervene over the economy activities of the firms and households.

5. National income = national product: rate of interest or the level of income of the people does not determine the investment. The model assumes that all net investment is made autonomously.

6. **Figure 2.4.1. Two sector Model: Flow Chart**

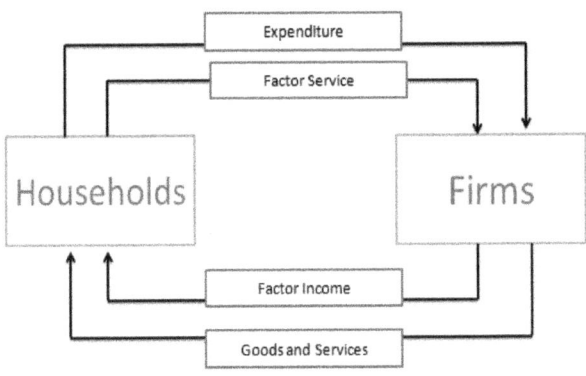

1. The above diagram shows that there are circular broken lines that represent the flow of the factors and products and represent real flows.

2. The continuous lines which are not broken or dotted represent the money flows which are generated as a result of the real flows.

3. The arrows point the direction in which the flow happens. It can be seen in the diagram that the two flows, the real flows and the money flows travelled in opposite directions.

4. In the model, the total value of real flows equals the money flows as it is assumed that factor payments are always equal to the incomes of the households.

5. The income of the household is entirely spent on the services and the goods that are manufactured / provided by the firms. Due to this, the expenditures of the household are always equal to the total earnings which is also equal to the value of the entire output of the firms.

6. Therefore mathematically,

The value of output= household incomes= household expenditure= total earnings of the firms.

7. The model implicates that expenses made by the households become the source of earnings for the manufacturers of the service providers and vice versa.

8. The firms provide payment to the factor owners for providing the factors of production, and the factor owners spend this money on the goods and services produced by the industries.

9. This causes a state of equilibrium in which the earnings of the manufacturers are service providers equals to the incomes of the households which equals to the consumption expenditure by the households. In the state of equilibrium, the total demand equals total supply in the economy.

10. This process is continuous and leads to an equalisation in the GNP (Gross National Product) and GNI (Gross National income*).

(*Gross national income is the value of all income produced by a country's residents within its geographical borders.)

2.5. Measurement of National Income:

National income is the aggregate of the current achievements of an economy for a given year. It represents the net monitory value of all the services and goods produced by the entire economy over a period of one year. As far as measurement of national income is concerned, the following are the methods of measuring national income:

1. Income method of measuring national income:

Under this method, the national income is measured as a flow of factor incomes. Land, labour, capital et cetera are the factors of production which produce income. Under the income approach of measuring national income, all the incomes of all the factors of production (before taxation) within an economy are summed up for a particular year. This approach is also called as income distributed approach. Income that does not arise from productive activities such as sickness benefits, compensation received for an accidents et cetera is not included for the calculation of national income under the method. The undistributed profits of the private sector and the surplus of the public sector enterprises is included while calculating national income under this method. Transfer payments made by the government and goods and services for which monetary consideration is not paid are not included in the calculation of national income under this method. The major assumption of this method is that the income earned by the various factors of production is equal to the monetary value of the services and goods produced during the entire year. To sum up, the following are the components of national income according to the income approach:

1. Compensation of the employees (which includes salaries and wages in cash, salaries and wages in kind perquisites, contribution of the employees to social security schemes such as provident fund gratuity et cetera)
2. Rent for the land and building.
3. Royalties that are received by different means such as leasing of coal mines, iron mines et cetera.
4. Mixed income (income generated by self-employed individuals who may be farmers, barbers, small shopkeepers et cetera)
5. Profits including retained earnings.

2. Value-added method of calculating national income:

This method is also known as the output method as it calculates national income by considering the value-added to a particular product during the various stages of its production. The net value at factor costs is calculated after deducting the net indirect taxes. This method of calculating national income classifies the entire economy into different categories of industries such as agriculture, communication, entertainment, transportation, fishing et cetera. Since this particular method focuses on the net value-added, the raw materials consumption, net indirect taxes and capital consumption excluded while calculating national income under this method. This method, firstly all the manufacturing units in the particular economy are classified into tertiary, secondary and primary sectors. Later, the gross value added is calculated by deducting intermediate consumption from the value of total output. In the next step, the GDP is estimated by adding the gross value added of the primary, secondary and tertiary sector. Finally, the national income is calculated by adding the net factor income from abroad and deducting depreciation and indirect taxes.

3. Expenditure Method:

According to the expenditure method of calculating national income, the expenditures made by companies, governments and individuals is added up. This method considers the overall spending by consumers, investments made by firms, foreigners, net exports (arrived after deducting imports from exports) and the spendings of the government to calculate the national income. Under this method,

1. The private final consumption expenditure made by households, non-profit institutions, expenditure made by normal residents in foreign countries for purposes of travelling.

2. The final consumption expenditure of the government which includes all expenditure made by the government on various services that are provided to the public. It also includes expenditure on services like education, defence and maintaining law and order in the country et cetera.

3. Net exports and gross investments made by the selected sectors in the economy. It also includes investment in inventory items made by firms.

4. Product Method:

Under this method, the total expenditure that is incurred by the individuals in the economy for a particular year are added up. The national income is measured as a flow of goods and services during a particular year. The method only considers final goods and excludes intermediate goods. Intermediate goods are those goods which are not directly consumed but are used for further production. The expenditure made by firms and public authorities as well as personal consumption expenditure is included for the purpose of calculating national income under this method. In this method, the entire economy is divided into different sectors and the total products produced by these sectors are added up. This helps in understanding the contribution of each sector to the national income. The government can use this method of calculating national income to understand the need for development of certain sectors and can increase the output generated by the sectors by designing specific policies for them.

2.6. Importance of National Income Analysis.

The national income is generally one of the most important statistics which shows the overall economic condition of the country. Whether it may be an individual or the government, both must maintain the account of their incomes on expenditures in some or the other form. This helps them to get a clear idea of what are the sources of income and the different heads of expenditure. When private individuals maintain the account is referred to private accounting and sizes the entire economy went into account it is called as social accounting. There are several reasons as to why national income analysis is important. Following are some of the reasons that underline the importance of national income analysis.

1. Comparing standards of living: National income analysis facilitates the comparison of the people's living standards at the international level. A particular country can compare its national income with the other country to understand the differences between the overall standards of living of people of different nations.

2. Underline the importance of certain sectors: It helps the government to realise the importance of various sectors and the contribution to the economic development of the country. From the point of view of national income, the government understands how the income has been earned, distributed, saved or taxed.

3. Building macroeconomic models: The analysis of national income helps in building short run and long-run economic models. Economics model economic models provide a theoretical construct that represents various economic processes by a set of variables and explains the relationships between them. It helps in understanding the complex processes that happen within an economy and also help the government in deciding the policies for the development of certain sectors within the economy.

4. Policy Decisions: The statistics of national income are important machinery for performing macroeconomic analysis which helps the government to make policy decisions. The national income estimates help in measuring the aggregate of economic activities of a particular country. This helps the governments to design short term and long-term strategies for sustainable economic growth and development.

5. Economic Planning: The analysis of the national income statistics enables us to get a fair idea about the overall structure of the economy. Without understanding the overall structure of the economy, economic planning is impossible. Short term and long-term economic plans are dependent on the national income statistics and estimates to a great extent. Without having the data related to the gross income, savings, output and total consumption from different sources, economic planning is not possible.

6. Budgets: Governments have to operate within budgets that are prepared within the framework of the data related to the national income. The borrowing and taxation policies are framed in such a way that they do not adversely affect the national income. Therefore, the analysis of national income helps the governments to set up budgets and bring about targeted economic development. The aim of the government while preparing the budgets is to formulate counter-cyclical policies based on the facts that are revealed by the estimates of national income. A countercyclical policy aims at reducing spending and raising taxes during the boom period and increasing spending and cutting taxes during the periods of recession.

7. Forecasting of economic conditions: By analysing the trends in national income, the businesses at the micro level can get help to forecast the future demand for their products and services. It also helps foreign investors to understand the current situation of a particular economy before making investments in it.

8. Understanding the income distribution: The analysis of national income helps the government to understand the distribution of income for various factors of production within the economy. This can help the government to solve the problems related to income gaps and inequalities.

9. Calculating other vital macroeconomic variables: Several macroeconomic variables such as the current account deficit/GDP ratio, fiscal deficit to GDP ratio, tax GDP ratio, debt GDP ratio et cetera are dependent upon the statistic of national income.

10. Facilitates inter-regional and inter-temporal comparisons: The analysis of national income helps the country to make inter-regional comparisons and inter-temporal comparisons (comparisons made at different time periods) of economic growth and development. This helps the government to bring about balanced regional development and put up a fight against the evils of poverty and unemployment.

2.7. Difficulties in the measurement of national income:

The difficulties in measurement of national income can be classified under two broad categories as follows:

A. Conceptual difficulties

B. Statistical difficulties

A. Conceptual difficulties:

1. Absence of a concrete definition of national income: there is absence of a universal definition for calculating national income. This creates doubts about which things must be included or excluded by calculating the national income for a particular economy.

2. Services that are rendered without remuneration: for the purpose of calculating national income, services that are rendered without any consideration remuneration are not considered. For example, the services of a father or mother to the household are productive but cannot be counted in terms of money. Therefore, the major problem with the calculation of national income is that it does not consider such products and services that are rendered without consideration remuneration.

3. Differentiating intermediate and final goods: while calculating the national income for a particular country, only the value of final goods and services is considered. Final goods of those goods which are produced for the purpose of consumption. When national income is estimated, it is not always feasible to draw a clear line that distinguishes final goods and intermediate goods. For instance, cotton used at dispensary for cleaning a wound is the final product for the medical practitioner, but if the same cotton is used for manufacturing a garment, it will be treated as an intermediate product.

4. Transfer payments: transfer payments are those payments for which the receiver of such a payment need not perform any economic activity. For example, if a mother gives her child some pocket money, or the government pays pension to the employees who have retired from the services, there is no economic activity involved on the part of the receiver. Such transfer payments are sources of income for the firms and households; these are not included as a part of the national income.

5. Pricing of the products: It is a very difficult job to value the final products and services for the purpose of estimating national income. The nature of the market is dynamic, and prices change every single day. The prices for goods and services are determined by the demand and supply forces that are acting in the market. This leaves us with a big lacuna as to which prize should be chosen to ascertain the exact monetary value of products and services? There are different prices that exist in the market which are wholesale price or retail price et cetera. It is difficult to decide as to which prices must be used for the purpose of finding of the monetary value of the final goods and services.

6. Income of the non-domestic companies: the income which the foreign firms retained in the country should be included in the national income according to some experts. Experts also proposed that, the income which is owned by foreign firms within the country but repatriated by the foreign firms to the own countries should not be included in the calculation of national income. This issue is quite controversial and has caused several debates. This shows the very unstable nature of the concept of national income.

B. **Statistical difficulties:**

1. Data reliability: In case of developing and underdeveloped nations, majority of the people do not understand the importance and relevance of income data. People were living below the poverty line do not maintain proper records of the income. In certain cases, in order to avoid payment of taxes, individuals deliberately given wrong information about the income is. The people who collect classify and analyse income data must have the required skills and qualifications to collect the data flawlessly in order to arrive at an estimate of national income that is trustworthy. Investigators are any moderators were included in the process of calculating national income create distortions by introducing the element of personal bias and prejudice in the calculations. If the data that is collected is not reliable, the national income estimation will also go wrong.

2. Impact of illiteracy and ignorance: In some underdeveloped nations, several people are illiterate, ignorant and uneducated. They do not maintain proper account that can give a person any idea about the income and expenditure. They are completely ignorant about the aspects of accounting mainly because their incomes are very low. Due to this habit of not maintaining proper account, the contribution to national income of such individuals cannot be taken into consideration.

3. Occupational classification: In some underdeveloped countries, most of the people earn their living from more than one sources of income. For example, Indian farmers whose primary activity is agriculture may also be involved in a part-time job in some industrial unit when they are not actively farming due to seasonal constraints. As far as classification is concerned it is difficult to determine as to whether they should be treated as people were working in the agricultural sector or industry workers? While categorising them, it becomes difficult for the policymakers to classify them into one particular category. Therefore, when people have more than one sources of income, it becomes difficult to understand me source of income and a large part of such an income gets unaccounted for while calculating national income.

4. Problems with the nonmonetary sector: In some countries even today, the barter system is followed-especially in the rural parts of the country's the goods in exchange for goods. Violation of such goods which have been exchanged using the barter system is difficult since such goods never make it to the market. Therefore, the value of such goods is excluded from the calculation of national income.

5. Production for the purpose of self-consumption: For example, if a particular baker produces a loaf of bread that is to be sold to a consumer it would be treated as a final good. But he produces the same loaf of bread to be consumed by his own family, it will not be treated as a final good as it has been produced for the purpose of self-consumption. Similarly, there are huge number of farmers who produce goods for subsistence purposes. There were left with no marketable surplus and the value of such goods cannot be completed because they never make it to the market for the purpose of sale. Hence, the statistical organisations were involved in the process of calculating national income had to rely on guesswork which can be inaccurate most of the times.

6. Consumption of fixed capital: In order to arrive at the rally of the net national product, which depreciation costs from the gross national product (GNP). It is quite challenging to measure the correct value of the amount of capital consumed (ranked, machinery, buildings, land) during the year. Depreciation is calculated according to the rates that have been decided by the different statutory authorities in the country. This introduces the element of randomness (or arbitrariness) in the calculation of the depreciation amounts. This in itself makes the very calculation of the national income are murky process.

7. The problems of double counting: several goods and services may appear more than once in the national income estimation. It is very difficult to distinguish between intermediate and final goods due to which there will be double counting causing distortions in the calculation of national income.

8. Valuation of new goods at constant prices: When a particular commodity produced for the first time it is easy to know the price of such a commodity. However, it is difficult to find out is constant price. For example, in India we cannot determine the value of a laptop at the constant price of 1970-71, as a laptop was never being produced in that particular year. (The laptop was invented by Adam Osborne in 1981). Therefore, valuation of new goods at constant prices creates additional difficulties in the calculation of national income estimates.

2.8. Questions:

1. What do you mean by national income? State its importance.
2. Explain the meaning of gross national product at factor cost at market prices.
3. Explain in detail diagram, the circular flow of income in the two-sector model.
4. What is national income? What are the difficulties in measuring national income?
5. Explain the concept of national income. How is national income measured?

Chapter 3

Theories of Output and Employment.

3.1. Introduction:

Several classical economists have made attempts to develop theories related to employment. David Ricardo, Alfred Marshall, Edgeworth, Pareto, ACP Pigou, Adam Smith and JB Say are some of the economists who have made a significant contribution to the classical theory of employment. According to the classical economists, there is always full employment in the economy, and they believed the economy to be a Laissez-faire economy (which means of free enterprise economy.) The term Laissez-faire is of French origin which literally means being left alone. It means that in these economies there was very less government intervention in the matters of the firms and individuals. John Maynard Keynes heavily criticised the classical theories of employment that were put up by several classical economists mentioned earlier. He believed that the theories that were introduced in the 18th century were obsolete and could not provide solutions to the evils of unemployment during the great depression that happened during the period 1929 to 1934. Overall, the theories of output and employment can be categorised into Keynesian theories and other classical theories of employment. A systematic theory of employment was needed to be developed which could explain the very subject matter of unemployment and provide sustainable solutions to solve the problems.

There are different theories of output and employment, which explain how economy grows through generating output and employment.

Monetarist theory: Developed by Milton Friedman, the monetarist theory emphasizes the importance of monetary policy in managing the economy. Monetarists believe that the economy tends towards a natural rate of unemployment, and that excessive government spending and inflation can lead to long-term economic problems.

New Classical theory: Developed in the 1970s and 1980s, the new classical theory emphasizes the importance of expectations and information in determining economic outcomes. According to new classical economists, individuals and firms have rational expectations, and markets are efficient and self-correcting.

New Keynesian theory: Developed in the 1980s and 1990s, the new Keynesian theory combines elements of Keynesian and neoclassical economics. It emphasizes the role of market imperfections, such as price stickiness and imperfect competition, in causing unemployment and inflation. The new Keynesian theory supports the use of monetary and fiscal policy to stabilize the economy.

Overall, these theories of output and employment have different implications for economic policy and the role of government in the economy. They have been subject to ongoing debate and refinement as economists seek to better understand the workings of the economy.

3.2. The classical theory of employment:

Laissez-fair However according to Keynes, he defined classical economists as the people who follow David Ricardo including Alfred Marshall, John Stuart Mill and Pigou. Keynes regards the principles of classical economics as Orthodox. Keynes was an ardent follower of Alfred Marshall and had accepted and also taught these classical principles. Yet, he was the major features of the classical theory of employment were that the classical theory assumed full employment of labour and other productive resources. It also assumed the flexibility of prices and wages to bring about full employment.

As per classical economists, the economy is self controlled and tends towards full employment. Wages and prices would be adjusted to clear market and it's reflecting there would be no unemployment for long-term.

As per JM Keynes government intervention is important to achieve full employment. If the government focus on spending and monetary policy, then it will reflect on aggregate demand and its lead toward full employment.

3.2.1. Full employment:

According to traditional economics, the economy always uses all of its resources, including manpower. According to traditional economics, if all resources, including labour, are fully used, universal overproduction and general unemployment are impossible. This is undoubtedly a hypothetical scenario that will never occur under real-world conditions. If there is any unemployment in the nation, it is considered anomalous or entirely transient in nature, according to classical economics. According to the traditional conception of employment, there is always a tendency towards full employment in a given economy and neither unemployment nor its persistence can last for an extended period of time. The following were cited as causes of unemployment by classical economists:

1. When the government intervenes or there is private monopoly, unemployment is bound to happen according to the classical economists.

2. Wrong estimations by entrepreneurs and incorrect decisions.

3. Artificial resistance offered by individuals get employed.

The economy self-adjusts in a properly competitive environment, according to classical economics. In such an economy, the forces of supply and demand determine the relative worth of products and services. The price system is the only factor that influences the planning process.

3.2.2. Flexibility in prices and wages:

The flexibility of pricing and wages was the second fundamental tenet of classical theory. This movie promotes complete employment as a result. Prices will naturally drop in situations when there is widespread overproduction, which causes depression and unemployment, leading to a rise in demand. As a result of the circumstance, prices would begin to rise gradually and productive activity would be sparked. The demand for labour would rise as a result of increasing productive activity, which would help to reduce unemployment to the point where it completely vanishes. A rise in labour demand would result from lower pay since more goods and services could be produced with that work. Therefore, it was believed that one way to address the issue of unemployment was to reduce salaries. According to traditional economists, if prices and wages are free to fluctuate, unemployment would decline and the economy would get closer to a full employment of all resources. The role of money was largely disregarded by traditional economics, who saw it just as a means of exchange. They fail to take into account how the money component affects output overall, employment, and income.

3.2.3. Assumptions of the classical theory of employment:

There were a few other major assumptions made by the classical economists for the theory of employment. They are as follows:

1. Every person is rational wants to gain maximum satisfaction. The flexibility of wages and prices of goods and services.

2. The theory assumes everything in the long run.
3. The real wages and the money wages were directly proportional.
4. The wage rates, rates of interest in prices of all flexible and technology is constant.
5. The output of a particular country is divided between investment and consumption expenditures.
6. Absence of foreign trade (closed economy).
7. Perfect competition and a self-adjusting economy, in which the forces of demand and supply determine the prices of goods and services.
8. Money is only a medium of exchange and the quantity of money is given.
9. Labour is a homogeneous factor of production.
10. Laissez-faire economy- no government intervention.
11. If there would be any kind of unemployment, it would last for a short period only.
12. As far as the agricultural sector is concerned, the law of diminishing marginal returns is applicable.

(*Real wages and money Wages: The amount of money actually paid to a particular employee is called as the money wages. The amount goods and services which can be got with the money wages, determines the real wages. If there is high inflation, and the money wages of a particular employee are constant the real wages are bound to decrease. For example, a salary of Rs. 10,000 per month in a rural area in real terms is much higher than a salary of Rs. 10,000/month in the metropolitan city like Mumbai, where the cost of living is very high. J.M. 's Keynes strongly believed that money wages and real wages always move in opposite directions. We believe that the cost of living rises at a faster rate than the rate of increase in the money wages.)

Summary:

1. The classical economists believed that there could be a situation of full employment. In order to solve the problem of unemployment, a general wage cut in money wages would gradually drive the economy to achieve the status of full employment.

2. The labour market equilibrium: The wage rates would be determined solely by demand and supply of labour. Demand for labour is the decreasing

function of visit while supply of labour is the increasing function for the same. (Fig 3.2.1)

3. The goods market equilibrium: Savings are always equal to investment, and both are a function of interest rates. If the rate of interests is high, it would lead to a rise in savings/investment is and if the rates of interest are low the savings/investment would reduce. (Fig 3.2.2.)

In figure 3.2.1, it can be seen that when the wages are high, the demand for labour will decrease causing unemployment. When the wage rates are cut, the demand for labour will rise to produce more goods and services. Overall, the diagram shows how the forces of demand and supply curve of labour intersect to reach a point of equilibrium where there is full employment and condition where the demand for labour is exactly equal to the supply of labour.

In figure 3.0.2, it can be seen that unexpected increases in saving coupled with the reduction in consumption expenditures can happen at higher rates of interest. When the real interest rate declines, the savings also decline restoring a part of loss of personal consumption expenditures. On the other hand, investment increases which replaces the balance of the decline in personal consumption expenditure. The diagram shows how the interest rates play a significant role in achieving an equilibrium state where the savings are equal to investments.

Figure 3.2.1. The labour market equilibrium:

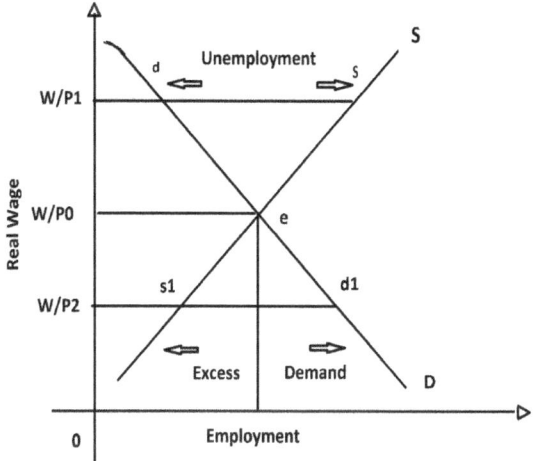

Figure 3.2.2. The goods market equilibrium:

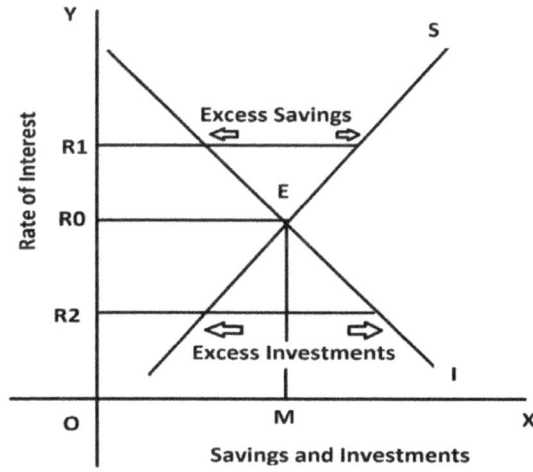

To conclude.

According to the classical theory, the employment and income are determined by the production function and the equilibrium between the supply and demand for labour.

The level of employment affects the production function. Here, the level of employment refers to the equilibrium of demand and supply of labour in the country. In capitalist economies, the classical economists believe the full employment as a normal feature and even if there is any unemployment it would be for a very short period and would adjust itself to reach a state of equilibrium. Therefore, it can be said that equilibrium is possible under full employment conditions only. This brings us to a discussion of the Say's Law.

3.3. The Say's Law:

"It is worthwhile to remark that a product is no sooner created than it, from that instant, affords a market for other products to the full extent of its own value."

(J. B. Say, 1803: pp.138–9)

The Says law lays the very foundation of classical economics. Jean-Baptiste Say, a French economist introduced the law in his 1803 book entitled "treaties on political economy". The classical economic theory states that the income generated by past production and sale of goods is the source of spending which creates a demand to purchase the current production services. The law emphasises that production is the key to economic growth and prosperity and the government should encourage the aspects of production. In general, the statement of says Law is: "supply creates its own demand".

3.3.1. Implications of the Say's Law:

The following are the implications of the Say's Law of Markets:

1. If a particular economy has higher number of producers offering a huge variety of products and services, it'll be more prosperous. On the contrary, the members of the society who merely consume the products but do not get actively involved in the process of any production will be a detrimental factor for the economy.

2. If a particular producer succeeds in the industry, it will automatically benefit other producers and industries whose output they purchased subsequently. Overall, all the businesses will be more successful when they locate near or do business with other successful firms. This implication also means that a governmental policy which encourages investment, production and prosperity of the neighbouring countries, will indirectly benefit the domestic economy.

3. Even if there is a trade deficit, import of goods and services is indirectly beneficial to the domestic economy.

4. If the government encourages consumption more than it encourages production, it will have harmful effects on the economy. According to JB say, consuming without producing enough would be detrimental to the wealth and prosperity of the economy.

5. Supply creates its own demand in real terms. Money is just a medium of exchange and is not of much significance. What matters is the real flow of services and goods for economic prosperity. Therefore, if there are changes in the supply of money, there will be no impact on the overall level of employment or output.

6. The law also implies that a particular economy should focus on increasing production instead of taking efforts to increase the demand. This is because, production is much easier to control and can be generated spontaneously as compared to demand. According to JB say, an increase in production will itself cause an increase in demand leading to higher rates of economic growth in terms of GDP.

7. In a capitalistic economy, there is unlimited flexibility due to the laissez-faire policies. Such economies function automatically by making optimum adjustments through freely operating market mechanisms in order to achieve states of equilibrium.

   The flexibility in the interest rates brings about equilibrium between savings and investments. Therefore, a major implication of the law is that the rate of interest is a strategic variable which can be adjusted in order to bring about equilibrium between savings and investments. The law implies that savings will always be invested due to which the aggregate demand would always be equal to the aggregate supply.

8. The law implies that if the production process is conducted under normal circumstances, the producers would not find it difficult to sell all what the produce in the market. According to JB say, work is unpleasant in nature. Since work is unpleasant, no one would work to produce a particular product without the intention of exchanging it for something of value. Therefore, all production according to JB say is done for the purpose of sale. When every single person in the economy is producing the products only with the intention of selling them, they would never overproduce as they would know the exact estimate of the quantity of the product which the others demand.

9. The law implies that all markets are money markets. In every single market, goods and services are exchanged for money. The only way there can be an

excess demand and supply for the goods is if there is an opposite excess of demand or supply for money. Indirectly, the law implicates that people supply excess goods as there is an excess demand for money.

10. The law provides that lowering the wage rates will lead to full employment under free and perfect competition. The law implies that the government should not interfere in regulating the wage rates and ensure free market conditions within the economy.

3.3.2. Following are the criticisms of the Says Law of Markets:

1. According to Say's Law, every dollar an individual makes is either invested or consumed in products and services. As a result, money is automatically spent at a high rate to maintain the use of all resources. Income is actually used for more than just investing and consumption. People save aside money for emergencies and circumstances when they would need a specific amount of liquid assets.

2. Supply does not always lead to demand: the great depression, which lasted from 1929 to 1932, resulted in a broad decline in demand for all items because people lacked the means to acquire them. Large stockpiles of finished goods accumulated in factories as a result of manufacturers' inability to sell their products. The stock should have been totally sold off since the supply would generate its own demand. Unfortunately, this did not occur, and the employers reduced the size of their task force and removed all job postings. More individuals were unemployed and dissatisfied as a result of this. Numerous economists have criticised The Say's Law for its failure.

3. JM Keynes noted that a decrease in wages does not result in more employment across the economy. This is because a sizable portion of the population relies on salaries as a source of income. The demand for products and services declines as purchasing power decreases. The economy's employment is not just based on income levels, but also on the total demand for goods and services.

4. According to Say's Law, all savings are invested automatically, and the rate of interest is a key factor in achieving an equilibrium between saves and investments. However, Keynes asserts that income is crucial in achieving a balance between saves and investments. Savings and investing decisions are more influenced by income levels than by interest rates.

5. Irrational presumptions: The legislation established a number of irrational presumptions, including consumer sovereignty, perfect competition, consumer rationality, and wage, price, and interest flexibility. All of these presumptions are false in reality. The Say's Law of Markets is less applicable practically as a result.

6. JB Say considered money to be neutral and only a means of trade. The fact that money is a store of value, however, makes it of utmost importance. Money plays a significant role in a number of economic activities, such as production, trade, consumption, saving, investment, distribution, etc.

7. No government intervention: According to Keynes, mixed economies—where the government may interfere and regulate or control the effective demand for certain commodities and services—are preferable. JM Keynes believed that the government's regulatory function was essential for the economy's overall prosperity. On the other hand, JB Say incorrectly presupposed a laissez-faire economy in which the government could not make any interventions. In actuality, the production of some commodities and services has to be regulated and controlled by the government. The economy will go crazy, there will be an oversupply of particular commodities and services, and there will be greater unemployment if the government does not regulate the generation of effective demand for such goods and services. As a result, the law undervalues and understates the role that government action plays in achieving economic success.

8. Long-term self-adjusting mechanism: Keynes said, "In the long run, we are all dead." Such a statement by Keynes demonstrates his lack of interest in and concern for the Say's Law's long-term implications. According to the law, overall consumer demand tends to be high enough over time to cover the cost of all the goods and services that a specific economy is able to provide. According to the law, the market's free forces alone are what lead to the long-term equilibrium. It implies the incorrect thing practically. In the long run, a specific economy cannot only rely on the automated self-adjusting mechanism to address the issues of unemployment. To boost investment and address unemployment-related problems, the government must step in and create particular policies.

9. Say's Law assumed that there was unrestricted, ideal competition in the economy. It is almost impossible for a free and complete competition to exist in the current economy.

10. Aggregation fallacy: In accordance with Say's Law, the rules that apply to certain businesses or industries may also be applied to the entire economy. The legislation implied the use of macroeconomic conditions to apply microeconomic concepts. Say's Law's assumption that microeconomic analysis may be extended to macroeconomic factors was attacked by Prof. J.M. Keynes as being incorrect.

11. The presence of trade cycles: If the aforementioned law were true, no economy would ever be harmed by the negative effects of trade cycle depression. Practically speaking, this is not conceivable because every economy has volatility. An economy must occasionally deal with the negative effects of depression, but it may also occasionally benefit from the boom periods that occur throughout trade cycles. Overall, it may be claimed that Say's Law did not place much of a focus on how trade cycles affect different macroeconomic variables.

3.4. JM Keynes' criticisms of the classical theories:

Keynes attacked the classical theories of employment and output because they were based on too many unrealistic assumptions. He criticised the classical theories based on the following aspects:

1. Assumption of full employment:

The full use of resources was a fundamental tenet of classical economics. This implied that they likewise believed there was no resource wasting. JM Keynes, however, questioned this supposition on the grounds that it was unrealistic given how frequently employment and output fluctuate in a given economy in a free market system, which results in a significant waste of resources. He said that being unemployed wastes time, money, energy, and other valuable resources. Second, capitalist economies frequently have depressions and booms, and investment levels can fluctuate significantly. According to Keynes, such economies often experience less than full employment, with full employment being the exception. He was therefore adamant that underemployment equilibrium—an equilibrium where there is less employment than there is demand—is a typical state in countries with a free market economy.

2. Government Intervention:

Keynes saw the need for government action in economic issues as a result of the underemployment equilibrium idea. The government must step in during periods of inflation or depression to create special policies and promote public investment. Government action is required so that it may create fiscal policies that will shield the entire economy from the dangers of extremely high inflation or an economic downturn. He blasted the traditional economists for assuming no government involvement. He said that the function of the government in resolving economic issues was totally disregarded by classical economists.

3. Keynes laid more emphasis on the idea of macroeconomic analysis:

According to Keynes, unemployment is a persistent issue that cannot be addressed in a short-term manner. Keynes argues that macroeconomic policies cannot be derived from the principles of micro-economies. Regarding macroeconomic policies that were drawn from microeconomic concepts, classical economists reached false conclusions. Keynes referred to these findings as macroeconomic paradoxes and sought to develop a distinct macroeconomic theory that could explain trade cycles and offer recommendations for actions that might be taken to attain economic success.

4. Keynes heavily criticised the Say's Law of Markets.

Say's Law of Markets states that because supply creates its own demand, neither universal overproduction nor unemployment exist. According to Lord Keynes, the rate of consumption need not be high enough to keep all productive forces operating at full capacity. Keynes contends that people's failure to spend or invest their current income in the economy is what causes unemployment. Demand cannot be created automatically by supply in a market with free enterprise. He thought the laws were unreal and impractical. He said that the legislation was written without taking important issues into account. According to him, an economy's level of output, employment, and income is always fluctuating, which alters the effective demand. When there is insufficient demand, there is unemployment. However, prices will rise and inflation may happen if there is too much demand in comparison to the supply.

5. Wage cuts cannot be a cure for unemployment:

Keynes was never persuaded that reducing wages would be able to solve the unemployment issue. Prof. AC Pigou made the case that salaries should be cut in order to promote employment. The classical economists believed that this was feasible because employees would offer lower prices to become fully employed. Lord Keynes, however, had a different viewpoint. Cuts in pay were not the answer, in his opinion, to lowering unemployment. He thought that lowering the pay would have a negative impact on workers' overall purchasing power. The total demand for goods and services will decrease as purchasing power declines.

A decrease in demand for products and services would also result in a decrease in the need for employment to create items or provide services. Instead of reducing unemployment, this would increase it. Keynes was also adamant that raising salaries is difficult in the current world. Labour unions are quite powerful and have a lot of negotiating leverage. The unions' negotiating strength was never taken into account by classical economists. In fact, Keynes frequently expressed amusement at the conventional wisdom that unemployment would disappear if wage rates were simply reduced.

6. Money is more than a medium of exchange:

According to Keynes, there is a connection between the "theory of money" and the "general theory of value and distribution." The Keynesian theory holds that money serves as the bridge connecting the present and the future. Keynes combined the theories of employment, money, and income while harshly criticising the mindset of traditional economists who thought that money was only an illusion. He thought that individuals save money for a variety of reasons. He is adamant that although some individuals save money for emergencies, others do it to take advantage of speculative chances. According to Keynes, money has a significant influence on income, employment, and output and is more than just an accounting tool.

7. Saving depends upon other factors:

According to Keynes, income level and capital's marginal efficiency both affect saving. He attacked traditional economics for holding that saving relies on the interest rate. He was adamant that if company expectations are low, a reduced rate of interest cannot lead to an increase in investments.

8. Laisezz Faire and self-adjustment:

Lord James Keynes vehemently disagreed with the notion that a laissez-faire policy was necessary for full employment to automatically and self-adjust. According to him, a free capitalism system cannot self-adjust since there are two kinds of people in such an economy: the affluent and the poor. When it comes to those people, they don't spend all of their money on buying things and services. This causes a vacuum in the overall demand, which then fuels an overabundance of commodities and, ultimately, an economic downturn. Therefore, Keynes was adamant that this government must interfere to alter supply and demand within the economy through the use of monetary and fiscal policies implemented at the macroeconomic level.

9. **Self-adjusting mechanism in the long run:**

Keynes said, "In the end, we're all going to die." Such a statement by Keynes demonstrates his lack of interest in and concern for the Say's Law's long-term implications. According to the law, overall consumer demand tends to be high enough over time to cover the cost of all the goods and services that a specific economy is able to provide. According to the law, the market's free forces alone are what lead to the long-term equilibrium. It implies the incorrect thing practically. In the long run, a specific economy cannot only rely on the automated self-adjusting mechanism to address the issues of unemployment. The government must step in and create specific measures to boost investment and address unemployment-related problems.

3.5. Keynes theory of employment:

In his book, The General Theory of Employment, Interest, and Money, Keynes created a systematic theory of employment for the first time. This novel was released in 1936, a challenging year. The Great Depression, which lasted from 1929 until almost 1939, occurred during those years. Around 15 million Americans were unemployed during the height of the great depression around that time, and nearly half of the nation's banks had collapsed. The Great Depression was a terrible global economic downturn that started in the United States and extended to every continent. The unemployment rate was the largest issue the globe was now dealing with.

The fundamental elements needed to address the unemployment issue were ignored by the classical economists, who treated it extremely carelessly. The traditional economists believed that unemployment was only a transient phenomena and that, over the long run, a specific economy always has a propensity to march towards full employment. However, Lord Keynes disregarded long-term phenomena and advocated the idea that humans genuinely pass away in the long run. He offered a more pragmatic solution to the unemployment issues and harshly challenged the conventional beliefs.

We have saw in the earlier section of this chapter how Keynes attacked the conventional wisdom. Keynes was a person who was constantly interested in finding short-term solutions to the issues of unemployment and who challenged traditional theories for being predicated on so many irrational presumptions. Keynes asserts that employment is not a natural occurrence. He was adamant that government action was required to address the many issues facing a given economy.

The effective demand theory of employment is another name for the Keynesian hypothesis. The idea holds that unemployment results from a lack of effective demand for goods and services, and that the issues associated with unemployment may be resolved by increasing effective demand. It should be highlighted that Keynes believed that unemployment was caused by a lack of effective demand rather than a lack of aggregate demand.

3.5.1. Following are the salient features of Keynesian theory of employment:

13. Lord Keynes' proposed theory of employment is a broad theory that addresses all forms of unemployment at all levels. The theory addresses intermediate-level employment, widespread unemployment, or full employment. As a result, a wide range of issues relating to unemployment may be addressed by the theory that Keynes created.

14. The idea emphasises both unemployment and inflation. This is due to the fact that both circumstances have an effect on the total amount of employment. Keynes was profoundly affected by the significant inflation associated with World War I. Even though there would be a certain amount of unemployment as a result of managing inflation in 1920, he said that inflation in the United Kingdom should be kept under control.

15. Keynes never considered using microeconomic principles to address macroeconomic issues. As a result, the theory he created was in relation to shifts in production and employment across a given economic system.

16. Keynes' theory was founded on empirical principles, hence it wasn't ambiguous.

17. Keynes rejected long-term ideas; as a result, the theory was dependent on short-term economic factors. The Keynesian theory made an effort to analyse the short-term phenomenon of unemployment. He made the assumption that a number of strategic factors would remain constant throughout time and would experience very little changes in the short term while creating the theory.

18. Keynes disagreed with the laissez-faire economic philosophy. In addition, he did not share the classical economists' belief in automatic adjustment. In reality, he advocated for the government to step in and create policies to implement a number of reforms in the capitalist system.

19. Unlike traditional economists who viewed money as nothing more than a means of exchange, Keynes' theory accorded money unique importance. The traditional economists believed that money was neutral. Keynes was an ardent supporter of the use of monetary reforms at the local and international levels to address unemployment-related issues throughout his life. He was a great believer in the value of money. If one looks attentively, one will see that all of his main scholarly writings on economics contain the words money, currency, monetary, or finance, indicating that he thought money had a significant role to play in macroeconomic analysis. Keynes argued that economies are prone to change and that money is not neutral during depressions. For Keynes, money had a significant role in shaping both the long-term and short-term flows of output and employment.

3.5.2. Assumptions of the Keynes theory of employment:

a. Keynes assumed the phenomena of unemployment and output in the short run. The simplified analysis as he could consider employment and output as two variables that move in the same direction. According to Keynes, the problem at hand had to be dealt with focusing on the short period solutions. He assumed that the amount of fixed capital employed, and the techniques of production remain constant and the subject of negligible changes in the short run. He also assumed that new investments cannot change the technique, tools and equipment and the overall organisation in the short run.

b. Keynes assumed that there is perfect competition in the markets and there is a high degree of consumption.

c. He assumed that the prices of the factors in the product remain fixed in the short run.

d. He assumed that money is important and can act as a store of value.

e. Keynes advocated government intervention to reform the capitalist system. At the same time, he assumed that the government does not play a significant role either as a spender or tax receiver. He ignored the fiscal operations of the government.

f. Keynes assumed that the economy is closed and disregarded the impact of imports and exports.

g. Keynes assumed that the law of diminishing returns is applicable to the productive resources or increasing costs.

h. He assumed that the working class suffered with the money illusion. He assumed they did not understand the difference between the money wages and the real wages. A small increase in the money wages would be enough to motivate the working class and make them happy and they would never realise that the prices have also increased.

i. Press enter he assumed that there is no time lag between income and expenditure.

j. Keynes advocated that an increase in employment depends upon the increase in the aggregate demand which in turn depends upon the increase in investment and increase in government expenditure etc. when aggregate demand is equal to aggregate supply; at that point there is effective demand. In the short run, the level of employment and income is entirely dependent on the effective demand of goods and services. Consumption and investment help in determining the effect of demand. According to Keynes, consumption and investment depends upon marginal efficiency of capital and the rates of interest.

3.5.3. The principle of Effective Demand:

The third chapter of Lord Keynes' book "The General Theory of Employment, Interest, and Money" explains the concept of effective demand. The chapter's central idea is that underemployment and underutilization of capacity can coexist at the point at where the functions of aggregate supply and demand cross.

The amount of output and employment in a nation are determined by the effective demand principle, in accordance with Keynes. The intersection of the two aggregate functions of aggregate supply and aggregate demand is known as effective demand. The collective demand starts to work at this juncture. In other words, Keynes believed that the degree of employment was based on the short-term effective demand for a good or service.

Unemployment results from a lack of effective demand, a lack of investment, and a lack of consumer spending. Effective demand for the goods or services is represented when overall spending, or aggregate demand (investment expenditure + consumption expenditure), equals aggregate supply of national income at factor cost.

Effective demand is produced as a result of the equilibrium between aggregate demand and supply. This state of equilibrium shows that the company's owners tend to maintain a consistent level of output. The tendency of the producers at this level is neither to enhance nor decrease their overall production.

Arithmetically,

Thus, effective demand (ED) = national income (Y) = value of national output = Expenditure on consumption goods (C) + expenditure on investment goods (I).

Therefore, ED = Y = C + I= 0 = Employment.

The above equation shows that the effective demand is always equal to the national income while which is equal to the value of national output. According to Keynes the value of national output depends upon the expenditure of consumption goods and the expenditure on investment goods. The following diagram will explain the concept through a bird's eye view of the determinants of effective demand.

Fig. 3.2.9. The determinants of effective demand

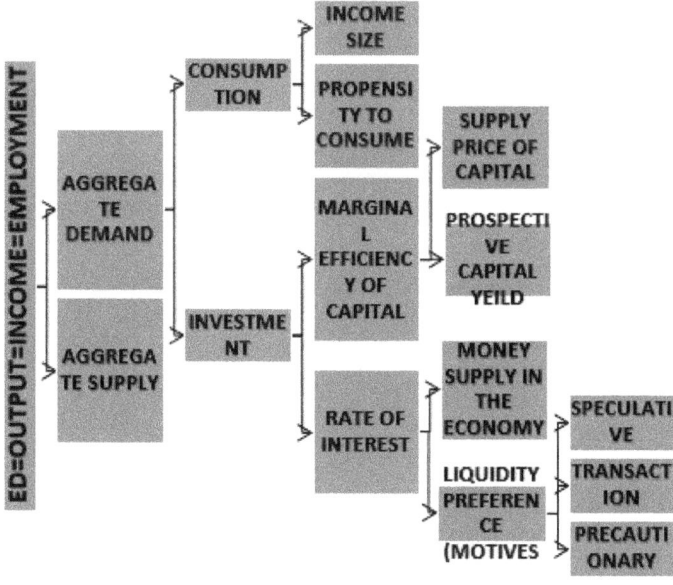

The diagram shows that how effective demand affect the total employment level for a given economy. It also has a major impact on the national income and the national output. The effective demand declines when there is a mismatch between income and consumption causing unemployment. By increasing the investment opportunities, the gap between consumption expenditure and income can be narrowed down. Effective demand can also be given a boost which can reduce unemployment to a certain extent. The next section of the chapter discusses the determinants of effective demand.

Following are the determinants of effective demand according to figure 3.2.9 that shows that shows the determinants of effective demand; the two major components are aggregate demand an aggregate supply. Therefore, we shall now discuss aggregate demand an aggregate supply.

A. Aggregate demand:

According to the Keynesian theory of aggregate demand, businesses only produce goods and services if they anticipate selling them. The potential GDP of a given economy depends on the availability of the various production components. The degree of demand for these products and services across the economy determines the actual amount of goods and services produced and sold (real GDP). If the real GDP is lower, changes in aggregate demand will also affect the gross domestic product without affecting prices at the same time. This demonstrates that the idea of aggregate supply has no bearing on the determination of real GDP and that the real GDP is solely driven by aggregate demand. This demonstrates the significance of aggregate demand in Lord Keynes's view.The aggregate demand price is the amount of money that producers anticipate earning from the sale of the product created by employing a specific number of workers. The level of employment and the price of total demand are positively correlated. The price of aggregate demand rises in tandem with rising employment levels and vice versa. In general, rising total demand results in higher employment levels.

Mathematical Formula:

$AD = C + I + G + (X-M)$

- Consumption demand by the households (C)
- Investment demand, i.e., demand for capital goods (I) by the business firms.
- Government expenditure (G)
- Net income from abroad (X – M).

According to Keynes, full employment is not a normal situation as stated by the classical theory. He strongly argued that the economy is equilibrium level of output and employment may not always correspond to the full employment level of income. According to him, a macroeconomic equilibrium can also exist at full employment. Keynes theory of determination of equilibrium income and employment lays focus on the relationship between aggregate supply in aggregate demand. The following diagram represents the aggregate demand function:

Figure 3.2.10. Aggregate demand function

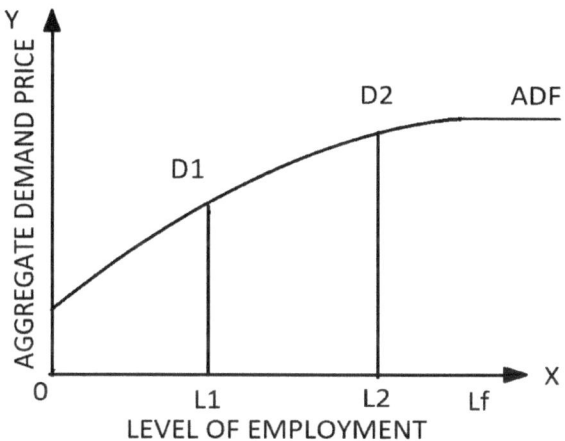

1. **The origin:** The ADF curve represents the aggregate demand function. It can be seen that the aggregate demand function curve does not start at origin as even at lower levels of employment, people would consume above their incomes.

2. **Increase:** The number of employed employees rises together with the aggregate demand. As a result, the level of employment (number of employed employees) rises from L1 to L2, and the aggregate demand function curve rises from points D1 to D2.

3. **Full level of employment:** While D2L2 represents the total anticipated receipts at the OL2 level of employment, D1L1 represents the total receipts at the employment level indicated by OL1. The complete amount of employment is represented by OLf.

4. **Sharp increase:** TThe graph demonstrates how the aggregate demand function curve increases quickly when employment growth drives up total consumer spending. Additionally, this raises the anticipated sales revenues.

5. **Ending:** As the economy approaches near full employment towards the end, the aggregate demand function curve becomes fully elastic and horizontal to the x-axis.

The link between the aggregate supply and aggregate demand curves is a key component of Keynes' theory for estimating equilibrium income and employment, as has been previously examined. He contends that at a specific level of aggregate supply, the economy's aggregate demand levels determine income that is dependent on employment. Therefore, one may conclude that Lord Keynes had a different view from the traditional economists who thought that supply generated its own demand.

The next section deals with the aggregate supply curve are represented by the aggregate supply function.

3.2.11. Aggregate supply function:

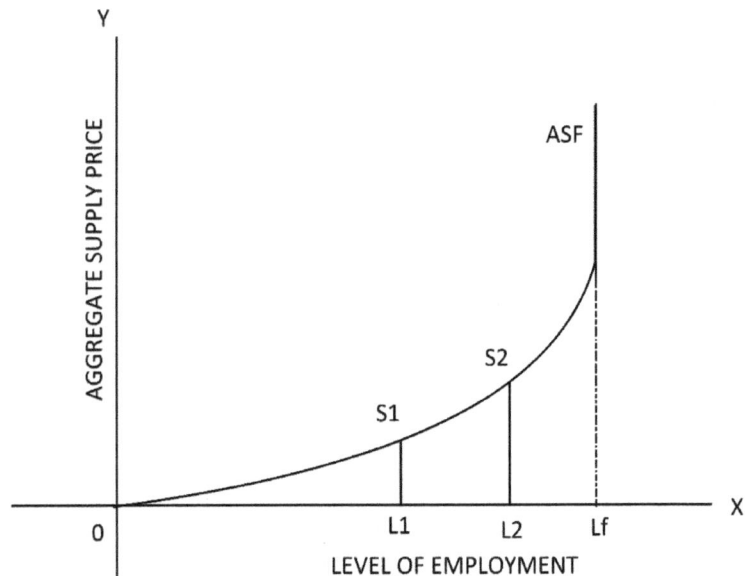

1. **Origin:** At the origin can be seen, that the level of employment is zero, and so as the aggregate supply price. This is because of there is no labour to produce any goods or services that will be nothing to sell.
2. **Progression:** In the beginning, the aggregate supply function curve will rise slowly as labour is available in plenty- which leads to a slow increase in the cost of production.

3. **About factors of production:** The aggregate supply is determined by the technical and physical aspects of production. In the short run, the technical as well as physical aspects that control the level of output remain constant in the short run. As compared to technology or machinery or other factors of production, labour is such a factor which can be adjusted in the short run. However, other factors according to Keynes remain constant and the output in the short run can only be increased by employing more labour.

4. **What is Aggregate Supply price?** The aggregate supply price is the number of total receipts which all the firms must expect to receive from the sale of output that is produced by a given number of workers employed in a particular process. It can be said that aggregate supply price is the total cost of production that is incurred by the manufacturers by employing certain given number of labourers.

5. **Increase in the aggregate supply price:** The aggregate supply price will increase with increasing the number of workers employed. The aggregate supply function curve rises and becomes perfectly inelastic at OLf are shown in the diagram.

6. **Sharp increase in the labour costs:** The curve becomes parallel to the Y axis and assumes a vertical shape perpendicular to the x-axis. The diagram represents that as the economy reaches near full employment (OLf), the labour cost will rise sharply.

3.5.4. Determination of Equilibrium:

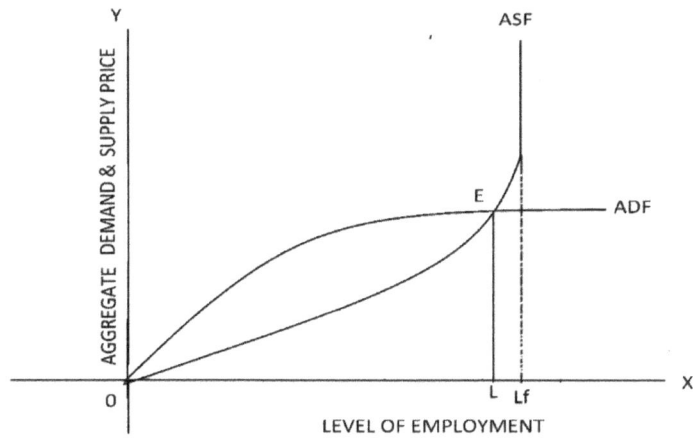

It is clear that the aggregate supply price function is less than the aggregate demand price at the level of employment OL. The manufacturers in this scenario anticipate increased profits relative to the cost of manufacturing. Therefore, producers would exhibit an expansionary tendency up to the OL level of employment, increasing the level of employment overall. The aggregate demand price would be lower than the aggregate supply price (ADF less than ASF) above that level of OL. The producers would anticipate lower returns than their actual production costs. The producers would rather decrease overall production. When employment levels are higher than OL, the economy has a propensity to reduce production, which in turn causes an indirect decrease in employment levels. The aggregate supply and demand prices are identical at the equilibrium level. (Where ADF = ASF). Therefore, neither a propensity towards economic expansion nor contraction would exist. As a result, everything is at an equilibrium level in terms of employment. He stands for the effective demand at that moment. The short-term equilibrium position is reached at point E, where the total price is equal to the total price of demand and supply. The graphic demonstrates that the equilibrium is attained when there is less than full employment.

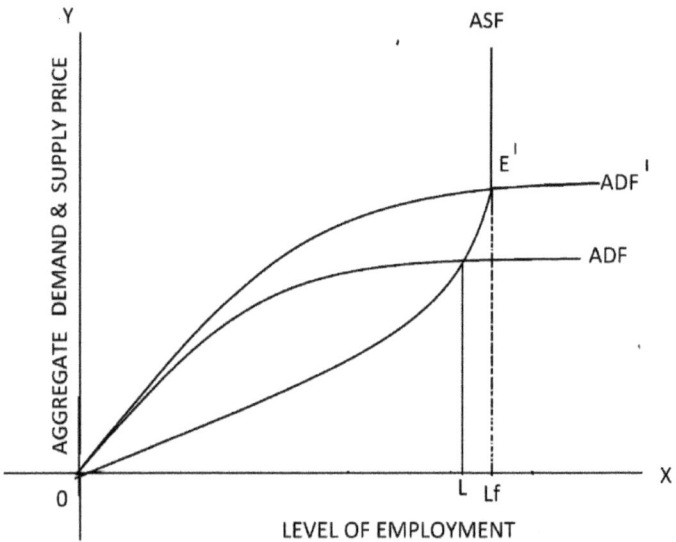

As illustrated in the picture above, an upward shift of the ADF curve to ADF' has closed the gap between the full employment level of aggregate supply price and the equivalent level of aggregate demand price. Currently, full employment is present in the economy at the point E', which stands for equilibrium employment at OLf.

Lord Keynes believed that by implementing an appropriate monetary policy that recommends a decrease in interest rates and a change in fiscal policy that suggests an increase in government spending, the aggregate demand function curve could be shifted higher.

However, Keynes thought that when there is an economic slump, monetary interventions will be less successful. Keynes argued that the government should step in and create countercyclical fiscal measures in general. He made the argument that the government must adopt expansive fiscal policies in order to avoid deficit spending in an economy that is experiencing a recession due to high unemployment and weak aggregate demand. Additionally, he suggested that during economic booms, inflation might be controlled by raising taxes or reducing government spending. Because he felt that "in the long run, we are all dead," he advocated that government should step in and address the relevant problems in the short term rather than waiting for the market forces to adapt themselves naturally in the long term. The short-term aggregate demand function may be turned into the following, in summary:

$AD = C + I + G$ where G is the government variable.

3.5.5. Criticisms of the Keynes theory of employment:

1. When Lord Keynes came up with this theory, those are the times of depression during the 1930s. Since it was more focused upon an economy suffering by depression, very less focus was led by Keynes on the concept of inflationary economics. During booms and inflationary situations within the economy, the theories that have been propagated by Lord Keynes hardly hold any good.

2. Suitability: the theories that were laid down by Keynes are not applicable to countries that are underdeveloped. The problems of disguised employment and chronic employment have not been properly considered by the theories that have been laid down by Keynes. In the case of underdeveloped countries, capital formation can happen only through saving. In order to save, the people should reduce the consumption expenditure. However, Lord Keynes suggested that there should be an expansion of aggregate demand and saving should be discouraged in order to solve the problems of unemployment. If people do not save, there will be no capital formation and the underdeveloped countries will suffer.

3. Overemphasis on capitalist economies: the theories that have been laid down by Keynes are based on economies that are capitalistic nature. Keynes neglects the socialist economic system even though he suggests government intervention to control capitalism within a particular economy.

4. Unrealistic assumptions: Keynes assumes a closed economy where there is absence of imports and exports. Keynes assumes that there is perfect competition in the market and that the government has no part to play as a taxpayer or spender. Such situations are practically not possible.

5. Keynes firmly believes that the worker feels better when his wages double even when the prices also double. Unfortunately, times have changed, and people have become more educated and economically aware. His theories seem to be obsolete and not applicable to the modern economic environment.

6. Keynes advocated that the budget deficit must be increased during recession. However, when the government borrows more the interest rate on bonds rises. With higher interest rates on government bonds, it discourages investment by the private sector. This creates an adverse situation and causes crowding out, which may be detrimental to the entire economic performance of a country.

7. Friedrich Hayek in his book the "Road to Serfdom" in the year 1944 criticized the concepts stated by Keynes regarding a centrally planned economy. If the government is expected to spend funds to prevent situations of depression, it is implied that the government knows what is best for the entire economy. This eliminates the effects of market forces of demand and supply in decision-making.

8. Keynes had misread the Say's Law, according to Henry Hazlitt. He had the opinion that if the prices are reasonable enough to draw customers, things can almost always find consumers. The traditional economists never denied that the workforce in the supply chain may go jobless or that the items could be sold to satisfy the market's current need. According to Hazlitt, Hughes was unable to admit that government involvement, which resulted in the empowering of trade unions and the virtual rigidification of many prices and salaries, was the real cause of the greater unemployment in Great Britain in the 1920s and the United States of America in the 1930s. Markets were unable to achieve a competitive equilibrium between supply and demand for a variety of products and services because of political and special interests. The market at the time was distorted by locked wages and prices, which had

a negative impact on employment and output prospects. This was the real reason for the despair that existed at the time. Given that Keynes primarily concentrated on macroeconomic aggregates and neglected to take into account the microeconomic interaction among a variety of different individual prices and incomes, Hazlitt believed that Keynes's attempts to fix information were both common and risky.

9. Keynes advocated aggregate demand only through to sector model which included investment and consumption. However, post-Keynesian economists introduced a more comprehensive four sector model which included investment, consumption, foreign sector and the government sector.

10. According to Keynes, there is no proportional relationship between income and consumption. However, several economists like Friedman, Hicks, Hansen etc. argued that there is a proportional relationship between income and consumption.

3.6. Questions:

1. Explain the classical theory of employment, what were the assumptions of the classical theory?

2. Explain the Says Law. What were the assumptions of the Say's Law?

3. Explain the Says Law. What were the criticisms of the Say's Law?

4. Explain Aggregate demand and aggregate supply and equilibrium with suitable diagrams as propagated by Keynes.

5. How did Keynes criticise the classical theories?

6. Explain the Keynes theory of employment, its salient features and assumptions.

7. Explain the Keynes theory of employment, its salient features and criticism.

Chapter 4

Demand for money

4.1. Classical approach to demand for money

Concept -

The demand for money means to the desire of individuals and businesses to hold money in the form of cash or deposits in financial institutions, for transactions and other purposes. Money is used to facilitate the exchange of goods and services in the economy, and as a store of value to meet future requirements.

There are different factors that influence the demand for money:

Level of income: The demand of money is closely associated with Income. Increase in income push to increase demand for money.

Interest rates: Interest rate adversely affecting on demand for money. If interest rates are high, people are more likely to hold their wealth in interest-bearing assets such as bonds or bank deposits, rather than as cash.

Price level: Price level is positively related to the price level, people need more money to do the transactions if the prices are higher.

Payment technology: Use of UPI, Credit Cards and digital payments can influence the demand for money.

Economic stability:

If there is uncertainty or recession in economy then people hold more money.

In macroeconomics, the demand for money is an important concept and it gives guideline to Central banks to manage the supply of money and interest rate to achieve their macroeconomic goals, such as full employment, price stability and economic growth.

Classical Approach

P = Price level

T = Volume of transactions

The money demand function can be generated by fiddling with the equation $MV = PT$ as described below:

$Md = PT/V$

Here Md = Demand for money.

The number of transactions over time multiplied by the average price level divided by the average velocity of money circulation results in the demand for money. This is a restatement of the money demand equation:

$Md = 1/V \times PT$

By assuming that P is equal to Rs. 16 per transactional unit, T is equal to 200,000 units, and V is equal to $8, the demand for money may be estimated as follows. The aforementioned formulas can then be changed to reflect these values.

$$Md = \frac{16 \times 200{,}000}{8} = Rs.400000.$$

The proportional change in the demand for money will be equal to the proportionate change in the price level, assuming that T and V do not vary during the near term. This implies that the demand for money will be immediately impacted by changes in price levels. According to Irving Fisher, changes in the total quantity of money in circulation are strongly related to changes in the general price level in the near term.

Ms. Fisher argues that the quantity of money available is always inversely proportionate to the amount of money sought. The Fisherian equation, which may be represented as $1/V = K$ or as $M = KPT$, demonstrates that the demand for money is a percentage of the total value of transactions. K is the proportion of the total transaction value that people have in the form of cash. The equal sign in the equation stands in for this percentage. The letter V stands for velocity, which it is the opposite of. If we suppose that the rate of money circulation is 5, we may determine that the demand for money is equal to one-fifth of the rate of circulation, or 20% of PT. The demand for money will be 8 lakhs of rupees if PT is equivalent to 40 lakhs of rupees; however, if PT rises by 50% to 60 lakhs of rupees, the demand for money would be 12 lakhs of rupees. Figure 1 depicts the Fisherian demand for money function. The Md curve's steepness is quantified by K or 1/V. The money demand curve is a linear favourably sloping straight line since K is considered to be constant. It demonstrates a clear correlation between PT and the demand for money.

4.2. Cambridge approach or the neoclassical approach to demand for money.

The Cambridge approach to the need for money was put out by Cambridge economists Marshall and Pigou and is sometimes referred to as the Cash balance method. Marshall and Pigou are both recognised as neo-classical economists. Compared to Fisher, these economists gave more weight to the role that money plays as a medium of commerce and as a store of value. According to neo-classical economics, demand for money refers to people's desire to hold a specific amount of cash or other forms of currency. The entire demand for money is represented by everyone's desire to keep the local economy solvent. The following factors have an impact on how much money people possess overall at any given moment:

- Price at the moment and projected changes.
- Interest rates at the moment and future projections.
- Wealth with individuals

These factors, according to neo-classical economists, are stable in the short term. The following is how the neo-classical money-demand function is expressed:

$Md = KPY$

Where, Md = Money Demand

K = The percentage of the population's total income that is retained in cash balances.

PY = Nominal national income.

4.3. Keynesian approach to demand for money

One of Keynes' most well-known publications, The General thesis of Employment, Interest, and Money, presents his thesis regarding the necessity of money. (1936). According to Keynes, there are three distinct reasons why people keep their cash balances. Transactional, preventative, and speculative are these three reasons. As a consequence, the three types of demand for money—transaction demand, preventive need, and speculative desire—can be distinguished. The total demand for money or cash balances may be divided into two categories: active and idle cash balances.

Active Cash Balances.

Transactional demand and preventive demand are the two types of demand for active cash balances. There is a demand for money in transactions because it serves as a medium of exchange. There aren't any further receipts or payments at once. Between successive receipts, there is usually a lag, but payments are still being made as usual. As a result, people must always have cash on hand to meet their everyday needs. Keynes contends that the primary reason for retaining money is the need for cash for immediate personal and professional interactions. Therefore, because of the transactional drive, firms and households accumulate cash. Their numerous transactional objectives are referred to be either business or income motives. The revenue motivation is also known as the home transaction motive. Families have cash on hand for regular purchases. The following elements influence how much money households need:The first is income level. Family income levels and the need for money for transactions are closely associated, which means that as income levels grow, so do demand levels for money for transactions, and vice versa.

2. The price spectrum. When prices rise, there will be a greater demand for money in transactions, and the opposite is also true. Because more money is required to purchase the same amount of goods and services due to growing prices, the demand for money in transactions will rise.

3. The expenditure trends. If a society's members were frugal, there would be less money needed for transactions. However, a society would require more money for transactional necessities if a significant section of the population was wasteful.

4. The Duration. If there is a long period of time between two subsequent income receipts, people will hold larger cash balances under the transaction motivation, and the opposite is also true.

In a similar vein, companies need cash reserves to cover costs such as supplies, transportation, payroll, and other expenses. Businesses require their cash balance, which they keep for commercial purposes, to fulfil these commitments. A firm's turnover and the quantity of money retained for business reasons are strongly associated; as a result, the larger the turnover, the more money is held for business purposes.

The entire sum of funds kept for business and income-related reasons serves as the transactional funds. Income determines income, which is stable in the short term. Income fluctuates only over the long run. As income grows, so does the necessity for money in exchanges. The following are some symbols that can be used to describe the transactional requirement for money function:

$Lt = f(Y)$

Where, Lt = Liquidity preference under transactions motive.

Y = Level of national income.

People often keep cash on hand to meet any unanticipated expenses. The amount of cash that people have on hand to meet unanticipated demands is referred to as precautionary demand for money, or money maintained for a preemptive reason.

Sickness, unemployment, death, accidents, and other unforeseen events can happen to people. The uncertainty of upcoming receipts determines the need for money prepared as a safeguard. It is fairly consistent and relates directly to income. Interest-inelastic and flexible to changes in uncertainty, the desire for money for preventative measures. The following symbols might be used to indicate the prudent desire for money: Lp is the liquidity preference for precautionary purposes, and $Lp = f(Y)$.

Since it is difficult to distinguish between the demand for money for transactions and precautions in practise, both demand functions are driven by income and are both interest inelastic, hence they are collectively referred to as active balances. The following are some symbolic ways to convey the desire for active balances:
$L1 = Lt + Lp$

We may restate the money demand function for active balances as follows: Because both transactional and precautionary demand for money is determined by income: $L1 = f(Y)$. In Fig 4.2 below, the need for active balances is represented visually. At income level $OY1$, you'll see that there is a desire for active cash balances. Demand for active cash holdings increases to $OM2$ as income level increases to $OY2$. As income fluctuates, so does demand for current cash balances.

Fig.4.2: Demand for Active Cash Balances.

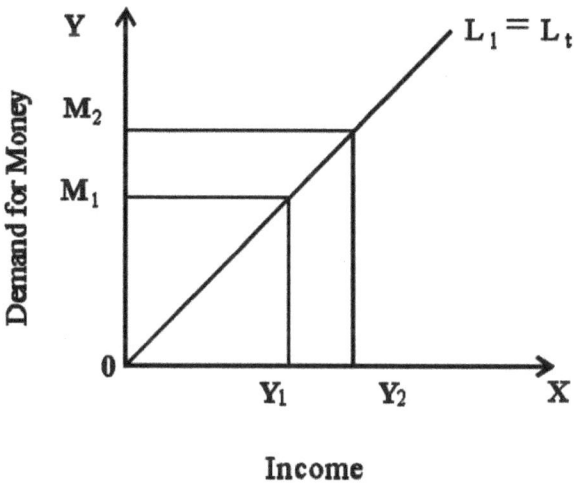

Income

Balances of Idle Cash (Speculative Demand for Money).

Investors' holdings of idle cash balances for speculative purposes are referred to as the demand for idle cash balances. The lack of faith in the future interest rate is the speculative basis for keeping cash on hand. Money is desired speculatively because it acts as a store of value. In order to benefit speculatively from securities investments, the speculator has cash on hand. According to Keynes, investors make financial profits through speculating on securities or bonds. The speculative desire for money is influenced by the rate of interest. The requirement for speculative cash reserves is inversely connected with interest rates. When individuals believe that the prices of assets that provide income, such bonds, will fall, the speculative demand for money rises, and vice versa. Symbolically, the speculative need for money might be stated as follows:

L2 = f(i)

Where L2 = Speculative demand for money.

I = Rate of interest.

Figure 4.3 below depicts the antagonistic relationship between the rate of interest and speculative demand for money.

Fig.4.3: Demand for Idle Cash Balances.

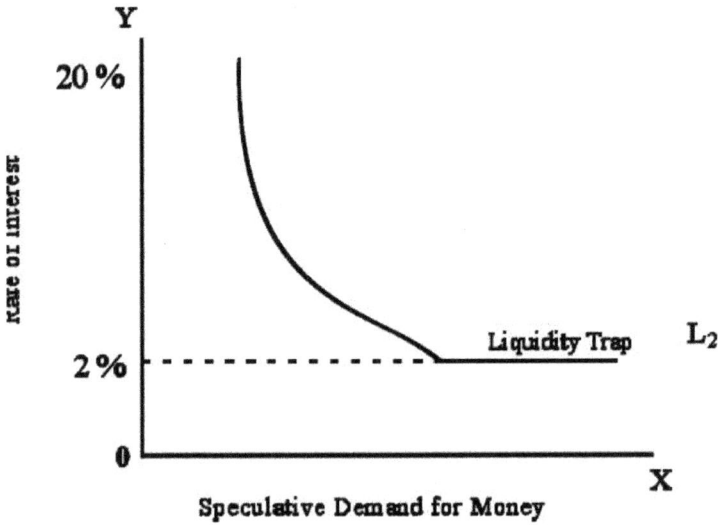

You'll observe that the interest rate and the speculative demand for money have the exact opposite relationships. When the rate of interest declines and vice versa, the speculative need for money rises. As a result, the speculative market's demand for capital is very fascinating and elastic. However, at very low interest rates, the speculative demand for money becomes totally elastic, which means that all income is held in the form of idle cash balances. This is due to the opposing trends in interest rates and bond prices. When interest rates rise, the price of bonds or other securities falls, and vice versa. The needs for money for transactions and precautions are income-dependent, whereas the needs for money for speculation are income-independent. When interest rates are expected to rise, people prefer to hold onto their cash holdings at the current rate so they can reap the rewards of higher interest rates in the future. When the need for money is rising for speculative purposes, there is a larger tendency towards liquidity.

The Liquidity Trap Concept

People store all of their income in cash balances for speculative purposes because the speculative demand for money is entirely elastic at very low interest rates. In a liquidity trap situation, the percentage change in the demand for money in response to a percentage change in the interest rate is equal to infinity. The liquidity trap condition is symbolically represented as follows:

$$\frac{\Delta M}{M} \times \frac{i}{\Delta i} = \alpha$$

The L2 curve in Fig. 5.2 at different interest rates illustrates the liquidity preference under the speculative drive. At an extremely high interest rate of 20%, the speculative demand for money is quite low, and vice versa. When the interest rate is only 2%, however, the speculative demand for money becomes entirely elastic. Any increase in the money supply or in income will now be held by the public as idle cash balances. The liquidity trap condition is depicted in the diagram by the horizontal section of the liquidity preference curve. At the current interest rates, the opportunity cost of holding cash balances is quite low, and it is projected that this opportunity cost will rise in the future, leading to the liquidity trap scenario.

Aggregate Demand for Money.

The aggregate or total demand for money is the total of all demands for money, including transactional, preventive, and speculative ones. The complete desire for money can be represented in the following ways.

$L = L_i + L_2$

Where, L = Aggregate demand for money.

The following can be used to express the functional relationship between nominal level of aggregate income and interest rate and total demand for money:

$L = f(Y, i)$

The liquidity preference schedule for a community can be obtained by superimposing the Li curves at each income level on the L2 curves. The liquidity preference schedule for a community is shown in Figure 4.3 below.

Fig. 5.4 Panel (A) shows a schedule of the active balances (the sum of transaction and precautionary needs for money) held by people at various income levels. Changes in short-term interest rates have little impact on active balance demand, which varies in line with changes in the amount of income. Li (Yi) uses this as an example to show how Yi wants active cash balances at his level of income, among other things. Li curves have a vertical slope because they are interest-inelastic. The speculative or desire for idle cash holdings is shown by the L2 curves in Panel (B). Speculators' demand for capital is elastic to interest rates and negatively connected with them, as you may remember. The L2 curve consequently slopes downward. At exceptionally low interest rates, the curve flattens down, showing that idle cash holdings are the only source of income. Panel (C) shows the liquidity preference curve, which depicts the overall need for money. It comes about as a result of layering the L2 curves on top of the Li curves. As a result, the curves L(Yi), L(Y2), and L(Y3) are generated, showing the liquidity preference schedules of the community at various levels of interest rates and GDP..

Fig.4.4: Total Demand for Money

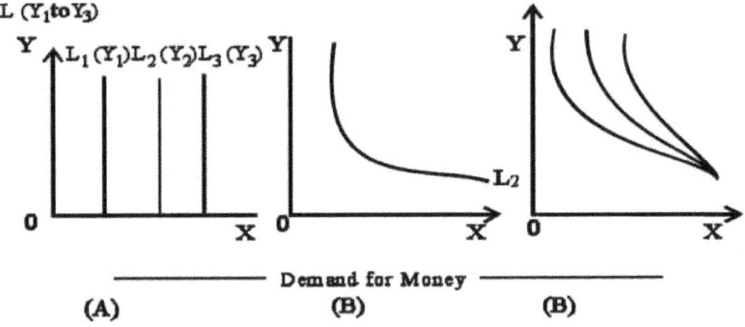

———— Demand for Money ————
(A) (B) (B)

4.4 Friedman's approach to demand for money

Along with restating the quantity theory of money and prices, Milton Friedman also put forth his new money demand function. According to Friedman, the money demand function is the most stable function. Wealthy owners might keep a piece of their fortune by investing in financial assets like money. When combined with other components of production, money, which is a capital good for enterprises, produces commodities and services. According to Friedman, people save money because they may use it to purchase goods and services. desire for money is also a desire for capital assets because money also provides benefits and services. The return on monetary wealth is the number of goods and services that may be purchased at a particular price point. Another class of financial asset that people can employ to accumulate wealth and get annualised fixed interest income is a bond. The interest rate on the coupon and any projected capital gains or losses brought on by changes in market interest rates are added together when calculating bond returns. The general public is also permitted to own equity shares and receive dividends, capital gains, and capital loss payments. People can have wealth in the form of investments and durable consumer goods, claims Friedman. But these commodities also offer returns in kind rather than cash, in addition to returns in the form of the projected rate of change in their values per unit of time.

The nominal money demand function proposed by Milton Friedman is as follows:

$$\frac{M^d}{P} = f(W, h, r_m, r_b, r_e, P, \Delta P, U)$$

By dividing nominal money demand by the price level, one can determine the demand for real money balances, which can be expressed as follows:

$$\frac{M^d}{P} = \frac{f(W, h, r_m, r_b, r_e, P, \Delta P, U)}{P}$$

Where, M^d = Nominal money demand,

$\frac{M^d}{P}$ = Demand for real money balances.

W = Wealth of the individual.

H = Proportion of human wealth to the total wealth held by the people.

rm = Interest income from money holdings.

rb = Interest rate on bonds.

re = Rate of return on equity shares.

P = Price level.

ΔP = Change in the price level, and

U = Institutional factors.

Milton Friedman asserts that the following elements impact the desire for money:

1. Wealth (W). Wealth is the primary factor determining the desire for money. In his notion of wealth, Friedman covers both actual and intangible wealth. Bonds, stock shares, and cash are examples of non-human wealth; human capital is a sort of non-human wealth. The money demand function takes into account the value of a person's existing and potential future wages as well as the non-liquid portion of wealth when calculating the ratio of human to non-human wealth as an

independent variable. The maximum quantity of money that a person can store depends on their overall wealth because demand for money is a direct function of total wealth. The need for money will grow as the ratio of human wealth to non-human wealth grows since human wealth is by nature non-liquid.

2. Rates of return (rm, rb, and re). These three rates of return determine the demand for money. Interest is earned on funds kept in savings and fixed deposits at the rate shown by (rb). The demand for money is a direct function of the rate of interest on money, meaning that the greater the rate of interest on money, the higher the demand for money is given other interest rates. The opportunity cost of holding onto cash is the interest you might have earned by owning bonds and stocks instead. As rates of return on bonds and equities rise, the opportunity cost of holding money will rise and the demand for money holdings will fall. As a result, there is an inverse relationship between the demand for money and the rate of interest on bonds, stocks, and other non-monetary assets.

3. Price Level (P). If wealth (W) is represented by income (Y), then Y/P, a fundamental determinant of money, generates nominal money income, and vice versa, a rise in prices will boost the demand for nominal money balances. Here, "Y" stands for real income whereas "P" stands for price level.

4. The projected rate of inflation (AP). P. As inflation rises, people will become less interested in holding money since their purchasing power would be diminished. If the rate of inflation is higher than the nominal rate of interest, the return on money investments will be negative. Therefore, when customers expect greater inflation rates, they will put their money into products or other assets that are resistant to price increases.

5. Institutional Elements (U), number five. The regularity of wage and bill payments is one of the institutional factors that affects the need for money. Furthermore, if people expect a recession or war, demand for money balances will increase. As long as the capital markets are unstable, there will be more demand for money. Politics has an impact on the need for money as well. All of these components have been considered institutional factors in Friedman's money demand function and are represented by the variable "U."

4.5. Tobin's portfolio approach to demand for money

A portfolio of assets that contains both bonds and cash should be maintained, according to American economist James Tobin, who demonstrated this in his essay Liquidity Preference as Behaviour Towards Risk in Review of Economic Studies Vol. 25 (1958). He assumes that greater wealth is preferable to lesser wealth. An investor should select what proportion of liquid cash, non-interest-bearing assets, and interest-bearing assets to maintain in his portfolio of financial assets. Risky assets like equities may also be present in people's portfolios. Given the risk profiles of various assets, investors can diversify their portfolio by owning a balanced mix of safe and hazardous assets. Investors demonstrate risk aversion, favouring lower risk over higher risk for a given rate of return. According to Tobin, investors are uncertain about the future rate of interest. If an investor chooses to hold a higher proportion of riskier assets like bonds in his portfolio, he will experience higher average returns but will also be exposed to more risk. A risk-averse investor won't pick a risky portfolio made up mostly of bonds, claims Tobin. Keeping just safe and risk-free assets, such cash and bank demand deposits, will result in an investor taking zero risks but also receiving very little to no return, which will prevent any increase in wealth. Depending on their risk tolerance, investors choose to have a broad portfolio of stocks, bonds, and cash, with varying amounts of each asset.

Liquidity Preference Function of Tobin.

Tobin was able to arrive at his liquidity preference function by establishing the link between the interest rate and the demand for money. Tobin predicts that when interest rates increase, wealthy people will be persuaded to hold less cash and invest more of their money in bonds. As a result, investors will hold more bonds in their portfolios at higher interest rates and there will be less of a need to retain liquid assets. In contrast, when interest rates are lower, investors will hold fewer bonds and more liquid assets in their portfolios. The demand function for money as an asset slopes downward, as can be seen in the accompanying graph where the demand for money is represented on the horizontal axis. This downward-sloping liquidity preference function curve illustrates how the demand for capital in the portfolio increases as the rate of interest on bonds decreases. Tobin calculates the overall liquidity preference curve by analysing how interest rate changes affect the demand for capital in investor portfolios. The viability of Tobin's liquidity preference theory has been supported by empirical studies on the interest elasticity of money demand. Empirical studies show that the aggregate liquidity preference curve has a negative slope, indicating that the majority of people in the economy have a liquidity preference function like the one shown in figure 4.5.

Figure 4.5. Tobins' liquidity preference curve

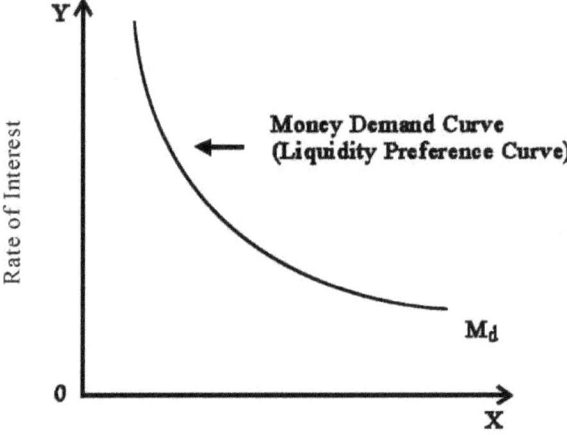

Fig. 5.5 - Tobin's Money Demand Curve.

4.6. Baumol's inventory approach to transactions demand for money.

According to Baumol, how business enterprises manage their inventories of materials and things is analogous to how money is required for transactions. Just as entrepreneurs maintain stocks of goods and materials to facilitate transactions in the context of changes in demand for them, people too maintain inventories of money since this promotes transactions of goods and services. However, maintaining item stocks has a cost, so it's crucial to keep an optimal inventory to reduce expenditures. Similarly, because it costs money to maintain huge sums of cash on hand, people should only have the absolute minimum quantity of money necessary for transactional purposes. The lost interest income is the cost of holding money for transactional needs. Baumol contends that the demand for money in transactions is not responsive to interest rates.

Savings accounts at the bank are mostly risk-free and provide some interest. However, people choose to retain cash and demand deposits on hand for convenience and to conduct their transactions. In order to cover the interval between receiving and spending money, people maintain money on hand for transactions. When the interest rate on savings deposits rises, people frequently transfer a portion of their cash holdings into these accounts.

The expense that people incur when they hold money, according to Baumol, is the opportunity cost of money, or the interest income lost by not depositing money in savings deposits.

Demand for Transactional Money

The demands of a person whose income is received on a regular basis and is spent gradually and steadily are examined by Baumol. On the first of each month, it is assumed that the person receives a paycheck in the amount of Rs. 24000. If he liquidates the cheque on the first day and consistently spends Rs. 800 daily throughout the month, he would have used up all of his income by the end of it. In a given month, an average of Rs. 12000 (24000/2) is kept in cash. In the first fortnight, the person will have more than Rs. 12,000 and less than Rs. 12,000 in the ensuing week. A typical holding of Rs. 12000) is shown by the dotted line. This is not smart money management because the guy is no longer interested in his financial pursuits. His money holdings of Rs. 12000 will be zero at the end of the fortnight or on the 15th day of the month if he withdraws only half of his pay, or Rs. 12000, on the first of the month and deposits the remaining Rs. 12000 in a savings account receiving 5% interest (see Fig.). He now has the ability to withdraw Rs. 12,000 on the 16th of every month and spend it evenly over the next 15 days (Rs. 800 a day). This is excellent money management because the person will be earning interest on Rs. 12000 for 15 days each month. The typical balance of this money management strategy is Rs. 6000.

Similar results would be obtained if the person decided to withdraw Rs. 8000, or a third of his salary, on the first of every month and put Rs. 16000 in the savings bank. He would lose all of his Rs. 8000 on the tenth day of the month. He can withdraw an additional Rs. 8000 on the eleventh to use up until the twentieth day, and another Rs. 8000 on the twenty-first to use up until the end of the month. To increase the return on investment, he will hold Rs. 8000/2 = Rs. 4000 in this new money management strategy and put the remaining amount in savings accounts.

Now, it is up to the person to choose a money management approach. The ideal amount of cash to store, according to Baumol, is determined by reducing the opportunity cost of frequent cash withdrawals (broker's charge) as well as the cost of lost interest income. Therefore, a greater broker's fee will result in more money being retained because fewer customers will visit the bank as frequently. A higher interest rate, however, will motivate consumers to keep less cash on hand for transactions since they will be forced to put more of it into savings deposits in order to earn a larger return. As a result, when interest rates are higher, there will be less demand for holdings of money.

Baumol's theory of transaction demand for money is undeniably an improvement over Keynesian theory, which maintains that transaction demand for money is interest inelastic. As a result, the transaction demand for money curve has a declining slope, as seen in Figure. People will carry less cash overall because bonds, savings accounts, and fixed deposits offer greater interest rates than cash holdings. On the other hand, when interest rates are low, there will be a lower opportunity cost to saving money and a stronger demand for money in transactions. Additionally, individual income (Y) directly correlates with changes in the demand for money in transactions. At a given interest rate, the transaction demand for money would be a direct function of income level and an inverse function of the interest rate. For the three different income levels, Y1, Y2, and Y3, Fig. 4.6 shows the three transactions demand curves for money, MD1, MD2, and MD3. With an increase in income, the ideal amount of cash to have on hand for transactions will increase less than linearly. Baumol and Tobin conclude that the demand for money for transactions is therefore influenced by both the interest rate and the level of income. MT = f (r, Y), where MT stands for transaction demand for money, r for interest rate, and Y for income level, is the formula for the transaction demand for money.

Fig 4.6 - Transactions Demand for Money: Baumol-Tobin Approach

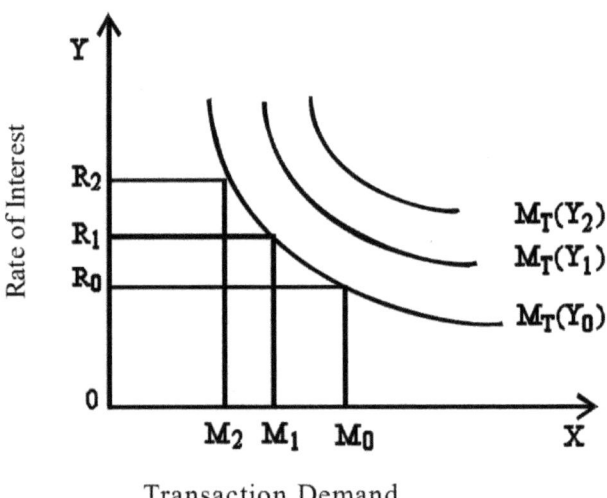

4.7. Questions:

1. Describe the Fisher's or the traditional response to the demand for money.
2. Describe Cambridge or neo-classical approach to money demands.
3. Describe the Keynesian strategy for addressing money demand.
4. Describe Tobin's method for dealing with money demands.
5. Describe Baumol's method for dealing with transactional money demands.
6 Describe Friedman's strategy for dealing with money demands.

Chapter 5

Supply of Money & Instruments of Monetary Control

5.1. Concept of money supply

The "money supply" is the total amount of currency in use in an economy at any given moment. It is the total sum of money held by all individuals, corporations, and government agencies other than the state treasury, the central bank, and commercial banks. The cash balances that the Federal and federating governments hold with the Central Bank and in treasuries are not regarded as a component of the money supply because they are the product of governmental administrative and non-commercial activity. The increased money supply is the term used to describe the available money stock. As a result, the money supply is the total amount of money in circulation. The money supply can be examined from two perspectives: money supply as a stock and money supply as a flow. Thus, the entire supply of money and the total stock of money are never the same. The amount of money that people have in their possession on a given day is the money supply when it is regarded at a particular point in time as opposed to when it is viewed as a flow across time. Financial units are regularly spent and reinvested throughout a specified time period. The annual average rate at which a unit of cash is transferred from one person to another is known as the velocity of circulation. The money stock is multiplied by the money circulation velocity coefficient to determine the money flow.

The entire amount of money that is in circulation in an economy at any particular time is referred to as the money supply. Physical money, coins, and easily convertible bank deposits are all examples of money.

Different sorts of money are included in the various metrics of the money supply. M0, M1, M2, and M3 are the most often used measurements of the money supply.

M0 is made up of all actual money, coins, and reserves kept at the central bank by commercial banks.

Demand deposits in checking accounts that account holders can quickly access are included in M1, along with M0.

Savings deposits, time deposits, and other less liquid deposits are included in M2, in addition to M1.

Long-term deposits, institutional money market funds, and M2 are all included in M3.

A nation's central bank acts as a regulating body, enforcing monetary policy using instruments like open market operations, reserve requirements, and discount rates.

5.2. Constituents of money supply.

The components of the money supply can be seen in one of two ways. The two methods are traditional and modern.

1. Conventional Approach. According to the conventional wisdom, there are two sorts of money: bank money, which consists of checkable demand deposits with commercial banks, and currency money, which is made up of coins and notes. The currency is regarded as high-powered money because of the State's legal backing. Each country has a central bank that has the only authority to produce currency in the form of notes and coins. The amount of money that is available in a country depends on the note issuing method that is used there. For instance, India introduced the Minimum Reserve System in 1957. The Reserve Bank of India is required to maintain a minimum reserve of 200 crore rupees under this system, which must be made up of gold and foreign securities. Out of this, the gold's worth should not be less than Rs. 115 crores. This reserve gives the Reserve Bank of India the power to print as much money as it wants throughout the country. Checkable demand deposits from commercial banks are used to satisfy debt. Derivative deposits are created through cheque payments, and this changes the amount of demand deposits. Based on the commercial banks' operations in generating credit, demand deposits are generated. Bank money is considered to be secondary, whereas cash is considered to be high-powered money. The popular wisdom holds that the two types of money that make up the total quantity of money are high powered and secondary money, also known as currency and bank money. The ratio of bank money to currency money is influenced by a country's level of monetization, banking practises, and banking development. In industrialised countries, there is a strong correlation between bank money and currency money, while this relationship is reversed in developing countries.

2. The modern approach.

According to the prevailing conception, the money supply includes both currency money and near money. The money supply is made up of coins, bills of exchange, demand and time deposits at commercial banks, financial assets, treasury bills, commercial bills of exchange, bonds, and stocks.

5.3. Reserve bank of India's approach to the measurement of money supply

The Reserve Bank of India has maintained that, in the strictest sense, the money supply is the total of demand deposits held by commercial banks and currency owned by the general public since the institution's foundation in 1935. Narrow money was given the letter M1 by the RBI. Broad money, also referred to as aggregate monetary resources, was first proposed between 1964 and 1965. Broad money was regarded as being M1 plus time deposits with commercial banks. In March 1970, the RBI approved the report of the Second Working Group on Money Supply. The 1977 publication of this study offered a thorough explanation of the money supply. Four steps to control the money supply were therefore implemented.

These four measures are as follows:

1. M1 = Currency with the public + Demand deposits with the commercial Banks + Other deposits with the RBI.

2. M2 = M1 + Post Office Savings Bank Deposits.

3. M3 = M1 + Time deposits with the commercial banks.

4. M4 = M3 + Total Post Office Deposits (excluding NSCs).

The Reserve Bank of India gives both broad (M2) and narrow (M1) money a high priority. (M3). Time deposits are included in broad money since they have some liquidity as they will eventually produce interest income; nevertheless, time deposits are excluded from narrow money because they have no liquidity and are assets that produce income. Time deposits have just been convertible, making them more liquid than they were previously. The M2 and M4 estimates of the money supply include post office savings and other deposits with post offices.

5.4. Determinants of money supply

Demand deposits and widely used legal tender make up the bulk of the money supply. The central bank and the government issue money, but commercial banks produce demand deposits. The following elements have an impact on the money supply:

1. High-ranking Money (H). High powered money (H) is made up of banknotes and coins created by the government and the central bank. The issued money is held in two places: the general public and the bank reserves. Some of the banks' foreign exchange reserves are kept in their own cash vaults, while others are deposited with the central bank. High-powered money can be produced by combining the currency held by the general people with the fraction held as reserves by banks. R is the amount of cash reserves of currency held by banks, Cp is the quantity of currency held by the general public, and H is the amount of high-powered money. The government and the country's central bank produce powerful money. (H). Commercial banks issue demand deposits, which are then used as money. To establish demand deposits or credit, banks need to keep cash reserves of currency, denoted by R in the equation above. Since they serve as the basis for several generations of demand deposits, which account for a sizeable amount of the money supply, these bank cash reserves give the currency that the Central Bank and the Government issue a lot of power. The connection between low-powered money and the money supply is under the control of the money multiplier. The ratio of the stock of high-powered money (H) to the total amount of money (M) is known as the money multiplier (m). The size of the money multiplier is determined by the currency to deposit ratio, denoted by the symbol K, and the banks' desired cash reserve ratio to deposits, denoted by the letter r. Therefore, if demand deposits remain unchanged and the amount of high-powered money held by the general population increases, there will be a direct increase in the amount of money in circulation in the economy. Banks' increased currency holdings won't immediately change the amount of money in circulation; instead, they'll begin a process whereby numerous public demand deposits are established in the banks. The amount of powerful money is determined by the Central Bank. As a result, its owners and managers, the Central Bank and the Government, decide how high-powered money will change.

2. Money multiplier. The money multiplier is the percentage by which an increase in high-powered money increases the money supply. Following are M = H.m or M = M/H. The supply of money is thus determined by the quantity of high-powered money and the size of the money multiplier (m). (H). The amount of the money multiplier is determined by the public's currency deposit ratio (k) and banks' currency reserve ratio (r), which together define the deposit multiplier.

The multiplier's size.

Demand deposits at the banks and currency in circulation (Cp) make up the money supply (M). As a result, the deposit multiplier and the cash reserve ratio. Demand deposits vary in response to shifts in bank cash reserves. The ratio of changes in total deposits to changes in reserves is known as the deposit multiplier, which depends on CRR. The value of the deposit multiplier is represented by the reciprocal of CRR, dm = 1/r, where dm stands for deposit multiplier. Dm = 1/0.05 = 20 when CRR is equal to 5% of deposits. According to the deposit multiplier of 20, there will be a rise in bank demand deposits of Rs. 2000 for every Rs. 100 increase in cash reserves with the banks, presuming there is no cash leakage to the general people during the process of deposit growth by the banks. Currency Deposit Multiplier and Ratio. Because the public does not hold all of its cash balances in the form of demand deposits with the banks, demand deposits and the money supply do not increase to the full amount of the deposit multiplier as a result of an increase in bank reserves. Customers might desire to retain more money on hand in the form of money balances as a result of banks boosting demand deposits in response to the growth in cash reserves. While demand deposits are being made by banks, some money is leaking from the banks to the general population. The amount of money that leaks out to the general public in the actual world reduces the rate of demand deposit growth and, as a result, the money multiplier's overall size. As the borrowers utilise these deposits to cover payments made by checks from third parties who deposit them in a different bank B, the process will continue. When cash of Rs. 100 is deposited in bank "A," assuming the CRR is 10%, bank "A" will lend out Rs. 90 and create Rs. 90 in demand deposits. Bank B will only have Rs. 80 in new deposits as opposed to Rs. 90 if the borrower from bank A withdraws Rs. 10 in cash and writes checks for the remaining Rs. 80 in borrowed monies. With this new deposit of Rs. 80, Bank B will create Rs. 72 in demand deposits, lend out Rs. 72, and keep Rs. 8 in reserves (Rs. 80 x 10/100 = Rs. The banking system's subsequent stages of deposit expansion are all subject to currency leakage. As more money is lost, the money multiplier will decrease. Therefore, a significant aspect in determining the multiplier's real value is the currency deposit ratio, denoted by the symbol "k". As banks' currency reserves decrease, demand for deposits will face a multiplier contraction, and vice versa.

Excess Reserves

The ratio "r" in the deposit multiplier stands for the required cash reserve ratio, which is determined by the Central Bank. However, banks are allowed to keep excess reserves. Excess reserves are impacted by the availability of cash, the success of investments, and the interest rate on loans to enterprises. The intended reserve ratio, as a result, exceeds the legally mandated minimum reserve ratio. Banks holding surplus reserves will therefore result in a decline in the deposit multiplier's value.

5.5. Instruments of monetary control

The monetary control instruments that the Central Bank has at its disposal can be separated into two groups: general or quantitative tools and particular or qualitative tools. The general tools are used to control credit volume in order to reduce pressures for inflation and deflation brought on by business cycles. They have a macroeconomic impact. The general instruments include the cash reserve ratio, open market operations, and bank rate policy. To limit the use of credit, the selective tools of monetary policy are used, and as a result, their impacts are sectoral. As a result, only some instruments affect the economy as a whole. Selective instruments are used to reroute the flow of credit to its intended and advantageous uses. Selective instruments include margin requirements, consumer credit control, directed use, credit rationing, moral persuasion, publicity, and direct intervention.

Quantitative or General Monetary Control Instruments

1. Bank Rate or the Discount Rate Policy. The "bank rate" or "discount rate" refers to the interest rate charged on loans obtained by commercial banks from the Central Bank. By providing discounts on qualifying recognised securities, loans, and invoices, the Central Bank provides financial assistance to the commercial banks. The purpose of the bank rate policy is to influence the price and availability of credit for commercial banks, which will then have an effect on all borrowers. The legal requirements that make the bills eligible for payment as well as the loan's term govern the availability of credit, and the cost of credit is determined by the discount rate or interest rate charged. As soon as the Central Bank alters the bank rate, interest rates in the economy change. The cost or availability of credit, as well as the demand for and supply of credit, can all be impacted by changes in the bank rate. In response to an increase in the bank rate, banks will raise their deposit and lending rates, and vice versa. A decrease in the bank rate suggests an expansionary monetary policy, while a rise in the bank rate indicates a contractionary monetary policy. The development of the money market, bank liquidity, business cycles, the evolution of the bill market, and the elasticity of the economy are some of the factors that affect how effective the Central Bank's bank rate policy is. If the money market where short-term loans are made available is poorly structured, underdeveloped, and made up of different interest rates, the purpose of modifying the bank rate will not be realised. Similar to this, if commercial banks do not ask the Central Bank for a rediscounting facility because of an abundance of liquid money, the bank rate will not affect market interest rates. Additionally, in order to use the rediscounting facility, the commercial banks must retain a sufficient quantity of qualifying bills and securities. If there isn't a robust bill market, the bank rate policy won't have the expected effect on money market interest rates. During boom-and-bust phases of business cycles, investment demand is interest inelastic; as a result, changes in the bank rate won't have an effect on it. Investment returns rise as the economy transitions into a prosperous phase and prices begin to rise steadily. As a result, investment demand will keep rising so long as the rate of return on investment outpaces market interest rates. In a similar vein, demand for investments would not rise during a recession when prices are falling even if the bank rate decreases, creating a decrease in market interest rates, due to the remote possibility of making a profit. Interest rates, costs, price, and commerce must all be impacted by changes in the bank rate. The economic system must be sufficiently elastic and responsive to fluctuations in the bank rate. Systemic rigidities will not have the desired outcome.

2. Open Market Operations. The buying and selling of government assets on a public exchange is referred to as "open market operations". In this way, the Central Bank can change bank reserves. When the Central Bank purchases government assets on the open market, the purchase price multiplied by the reverse credit multiplier is subtracted from bank reserves, and vice versa. The open market operation is a vital instrument in the Central Bank's arsenal for maintaining the general level of prices. The Central Bank selects its monetary policy options based on the macroeconomic environment. The central bank will sell Treasury bills, which are short-term government securities and long-term bonds, in an effort to control prices when there is inflation. The Central Bank will reduce bank reserves by doing this, which will also reduce the total amount of money in circulation. As a result, the interest rates on the money market will rise, which will reduce investor demand. diminish levels of employment, output, and income brought on by decreased investment demand will diminish the economy's overall demand. A decline in overall demand will help to restrain price escalation.

The free market sale of governmental debt implies a costly or constrained monetary policy. In a recession, when the central bank starts to buy government bonds, a loose monetary policy will have the exact opposite effect.

Let's look at the specifics of open market transactions in government securities under a stringent monetary policy adopted by the central bank. The Central Bank offers government-issued securities or bonds to traders on the open market. Then, the dealers sell them again to businesses, people, financial organisations, and commercial banks. The majority of the time, purchases of government property are made by sending checks to the Central Bank. For instance, Ms. Kareena will issue a check on her State Bank of India bank account in the name of the Reserve Bank of India if the Reserve Bank of India sells her treasury bills for Rs. 10 million. The Reserve Bank of India's balance with the State Bank of India will be reduced by Rs. 10 million when the State Bank of India pays the bill. After then, the State Bank of India will get the cheque from the Reserve Bank of India. By the end of the day, the Reserve Bank of India reserves held by the State Bank of India and the entire commercial banking industry will have decreased by Rs. 10 million. Selling government bonds for Rs. 10 million will reduce the amount of money available in the economy by Rs. 100 million, based on the reverse credit multiplier of 10. The money supply contracts in this way as a result of the sale multiplied by the reverse credit multiplier.

A few of the factors influencing the effectiveness of open market operations include the growth of the securities market, the rediscounting window provided by the central bank, the capacity of the central bank to assume risk, the balance of payments, the movement of capital, speculative activity, etc. Open market transactions, however, are seen as being more effective in managing credit.

3. Cash Reserve Ratio.

The Cash Reserve Ratio and the legal reserve requirements are two methods the Central Bank uses to control the movement of bank funds. Commercial banks are required to maintain a particular minimum level of non-interest-bearing reserves out of their deposits with the central bank. Although the cash reserve requirements are defined by law, the Central Bank has the legal right to change them. The reserve requirements in India were set at 3% of all commercial banks' liabilities by the Reserve Bank of India Amendment Act, 1962. The Amendment Act gave the Reserve Bank of India the power to set reserve requirements between three and fifteen percent. The central bank keeps a higher reserve ratio to control the money supply and guarantee smooth open market operations. The best way to control short-term interest rates is to have reserve requirements that are greater than what banks like.

The central bank can vary the cash reserve requirements to change the quantity of money that is readily available. The central bank may adopt a dear money policy and raise reserve requirements by a certain percentage, ranging from 3% to 15%, in the event of inflation. To demonstrate how changing reserve requirements affect commercial banks' capacity to make loans, let's look at an example. Assume that there are Rs. 1000 billion in deposits with commercial banks and that the cash reserve ratio is 5%. Commercial banks will have to maintain 50 billion rupees in reserves with the Central Bank. The banking industry will be able to create credit worth 20 times that amount, or Rs. 950 x 100 + 5 = Rs. 19 trillion, if commercial banks have excess reserves of Rs. 950 billion. The banking system will only be able to create Rs. 9000 billion, which is ten times its excess reserves, if the Central Bank implements a rigorous or expensive monetary policy and decides to raise the reserve requirements to 10%. As a result, when reserve requirements are raised, and vice versa, the ability to produce credit decreases. Since doing so would result in a dramatic rise or fall in interest rates, reserve requirements are never increased or decreased on the aforementioned scale in practise. For instance, a considerable increase in the cash reserve ratio will lead to very high interest rates, credit restrictions, a sizable decline in investment, and a sizable loss in both employment and national income. If the reserve requirement is currently 10%, it may be increased to 11% with a tight monetary policy and subsequently by another percentage point to 12% with a gap. Modifications to the reserve needs are implemented gradually and steadily. Under a cheap monetary policy, the Cash Reserve Ratio would likewise be slightly and progressively decreased.

5.6. Selective or Qualitative Instruments of Monetary Policy.

Selective methods of monetary management are used to influence the use and amount of credit available for specific purposes in specific areas of the economy. Selective tools are used to distinguish between various credit uses in various sectors, ensuring that the available credit in various sectors is utilised in the most beneficial and productive way possible. Margin requirements, consumer credit rules, instructions, credit limits, moral persuasion, and direct intervention are just a few of the different selective, qualitative, or specialised weapons of monetary policy. Here is a list of these resources.

1. **Margin Requirements.** The borrower must meet the margin requirement in order for the loan value of the borrower's offered collateral security to be determined. The loan value is calculated as the difference between the market value of the security and the statutory margin for that asset. For instance, if the margin requirement is 25% and the market value of 10 grammes of gold is Rs. 12000, then the loan value of 10 grammes of gold as collateral security would be Rs. 9000. Loans offered by commercial land cooperative banks require collateral in the form of equity shares, bonds, precious metals, and other financial and land real assets. The requirements for margin can be decided upon by the Central Bank of a country, which is the highest monetary authority in that nation. The loan value of a security might be affected either positively or negatively by an increase or decrease in the required margin. Margin requirements might vary widely depending on the type of security being traded. For instance, the required margin for equity shares in India is half of the market value, however the required margin for commodities might range anywhere from twenty percent to seventy five percent. Therefore, margin limitations have an indirect but direct influence on the demand for credit, even though they do not affect the availability of loans or the interest rate. It is a useful instrument for regulating speculative behaviour not only on the commodity market but also on the financial markets and the capital markets. For instance, the Reserve Bank of India has made considerable use of the mechanism known as the margin requirement in order to prevent the stockpiling of essential items and the subsequent increase in the pricing of such goods.

2. **The Control and Supervision of Consumer Credit.** There are a wide variety of long-lasting consumer products that can be purchased on credit and repaid in equal monthly installments. Some examples of these products include television sets, washing machines, refrigerators, computers, furniture, and automobiles. Consumer credit is regulated by the Central Bank, which determines the maximum repayment time, also known as the maximum equivalent monthly installments, as well as the minimum down payment required. In order to evaluate consumer credit, the Central Bank may decide to increase the minimum amount that must be put down, as well as decrease the number of equivalent monthly payments that must be made throughout the course of the maximum payment period. The initial payment, which is also referred to as the minimum down payment at times, and the installment amount are both increased as a result of this action taken by the

Central Bank. The Central Bank is able to reduce and maintain control over the demand for consumer credit by using these kinds of measures.

3. **The Issuance of Directives:** It is possible for the Central Bank to give verbal or written instructions to the Commercial Banks in order to manage the direction and volume of credit. This is done to ensure that the Commercial Banks' credit policy is in line with the aims that the Central Bank has set for its monetary policy. However, given that giving directives did not prove to be an effective method, the implementation of these policies now makes use of more direct monetary policy instruments.

4. **Limiting Access to Credit.** Rationing credit is a qualitative tool that commercial banks employ to regulate and restrict the purposes for which credit is granted to customers. Credit is limited in a number of different ways, two of which are the variable portfolio ceiling and the variable capital assets ratio. When referring to a cap that is imposed by the central bank on the entire portfolios of all of the commercial banks, the phrase "variable portfolio ceiling" is used. The restriction was put in place to ensure that the total amount of money borrowed through advances and loans does not exceed the limit. Because the central bank has the right to change the ceiling, this type of ceiling is referred to as a variable portfolio ceiling. In a manner analogous to that described above, the Central Bank may also decide the capital assets ratio for commercial banks. These regulations place restrictions on the amounts of loans and advances that can be made to different types of economic borrowers.

5. **Influencing People's Morals and the Public.** Moral suasion is the term used to describe the formal requests and persuasions made by the Central Bank to the commercial banks. Instead of issuing orders, the Central Bank is making an appeal to the sense of moral obligation that commercial banks have to carry out the objectives of the monetary policy. For instance, the Central Bank has the ability to request that commercial banks cease providing funds for speculative operations. It is a tool that is used for the psychological execution of monetary policy. By bringing to light immoral practises in the financial sector, the central bank has the potential to exert moral pressure on commercial banks. The Reserve Bank of India used moral persuasion for the first time in September 1949 when it urged commercial banks to take prudence when issuing advances for speculative purposes. This was the first time that moral persuasion was used.

6. **Action Taken Directly.** Direct action is a monetary policy instrument that can be used for both qualitative and quantitative analysis. If the credit policy of a commercial bank is different from the bank's monetary policy, the central bank may stop the provision of rediscounting facilities to the bank in question. If a bank's borrowings have reached a level that exceeds both their capital and their reserves, the bank may decide not to offer any further credit to the respective institutions. If a customer of a commercial bank requests an amount of credit that is greater than a certain threshold, the bank may impose a higher interest rate.

5.7. Questions

1. Define the term "money supply" and list its components.
2. Describe the methodology used by the RBI to determine India's money supply.
3. Describe the factors that affect the money supply.
4. Describe the tools for monetary control.
5. Describe the numerical tools of monetary regulation.
6. Describe the specialized or qualitative tools of monetary regulation.

Chapter.6

Dynamic Macroeconomics

6.1. Introduction

The core tenet of classical economics was that if wages and prices were allowed some degree of flexibility, then a competitive market economy would never fail to operate at full employment. In other words, economic forces would continuously be produced to ensure that the supply of labour and the demand for labour would always be equal to one another. The conventional economic model proposes that the labour market should play a considerable part in establishing the level of employment and income that is considered to be in a state of equilibrium. If the wage rate is lowered, then there will be a greater demand for labour. As a consequence of this fact, the demand curve for workers has a descending slope. The supply curve for labour is trending upwards due to the fact that there are a greater number of workers available at higher wage rates.

6.2. Wage-employment relationship

6.2.1 The classical theory of employment

It is generally believed that the notion of "Full Employment" was coined by the classical economists, who presented their thoughts on employment at the time. They have the misconception that there is healthy competition and that all of the manpower and resources that are available are being utilised. They contend that achieving full employment results in a balanced state of equilibrium that is representative of a typical circumstance. Full employment was defined as a state in which there was no "involuntary unemployment," however there is the possibility of frictional or structural unemployment, as well as voluntary unemployment. Classists were opposed to the notion that there might be a situation in which low unemployment and low aggregate demand could coexist in equilibrium.

They believe that real wages and monetary wages are directly associated since the majority of people who work are motivated more by the desire to increase their real earnings rather than their monetary pay. If wages were more flexible, then actual compensation would shift in accordance with the marginal productivity of labour, and this would eliminate the need for unemployment benefits. (MPL).

The following elementary tenets are the cornerstones around which classical theory is constructed:

1. Wage: Any increase in employment is linked to decreasing real pay, according to the MPL and the Law of Diminishing Marginal Productivity. This is the case regardless of the size of the employment growth.2. The Real Wage in Effect: a utilisation of employment that is only marginally inefficient. Therefore, the real compensation of an employee is the amount that is precisely correct to convince them to provide the quantity of work that they actually do. This is the amount that is known as the market rate. According to this concept, the workers' actual earnings are the most important factor to consider. The first postulate presents a timetable for employment demand, and the second postulate presents a schedule for employment supply at a variety of real wage rates (W/P). At the point where these two axes overlap, equilibrium is achieved since the marginal utility of the product and the marginal disutility of employment are equal.

6.2.2. Assumptions of Short-Run Classical Model:

1. The amount of labour that is available expands as real pay rates rise, which leads to an increase in the amount of labour that is supplied at higher real wage rates.

2. The demand for labour falls as real wage rates rise, which results in a greater number of people being hired at lower real wage rates and fewer people being hired at higher real wage rates.

3. There are no flaws or institutional rigidities; the labour market functions without a hitch and is perfectly flexible.

4. It is not anticipated that there will be a change in the overall demand for products and services.

5. Specific information regarding the demographics, preferences, and technologies involved.

The supply and demand for labour are what determine the equilibrium wage rate (wo) in the accompanying graph. The employment level is OLo.

Figure 6.1

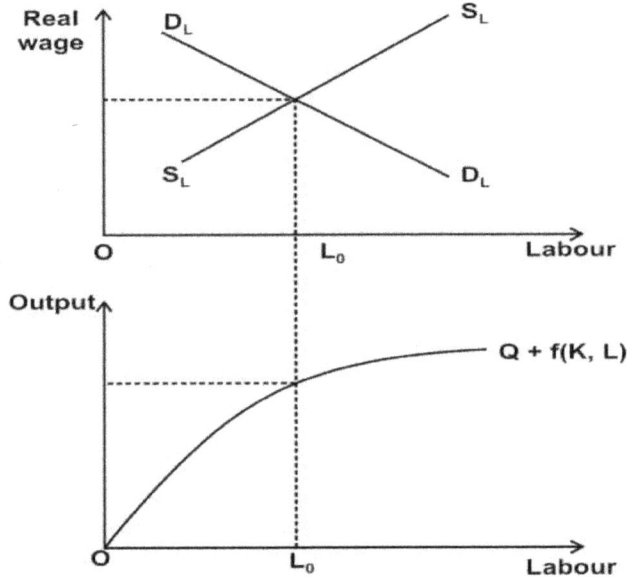

(a) **Say's Law:** According to Say's Law, supply is what drives market demand, which means that the only way to generate an amount of money that is proportional to the value of the things and services produced is to bring those goods and services into existence. When people participate in a barter system, where they produce (supply) commodities and seek other goods of similar value, Say's Law makes perfect sense. As a result, there must be a balance between supply and demand. In today's economy, it is safe to say that Say's Law is still applicable. The hypothesis of the cyclical movement of money hints at the existence of a link of this kind. For example, the amount of revenue that would be created from the sale of products would be just right to satisfy the demand for such products.

(b) **Saving-Investment Equality:** There is a significant problem with Say's Law. If the people who receive income in this simple model set aside some of the money they make, consumption expenditure will be lower than total output, and supply will no longer drive demand on its own. As a consequence, there would be an increase in the number of products that were not sold, a decline in prices, a reduction in output, unemployment, and a decrease in profits.Classical economists, on the other hand, did not consider this a viable option since they believed that firms would invest any money that households set aside for savings. In other words, there would be investment in order to make up for any consumption gap created by savings leakage, and this gap would be filled by investing. Therefore, Say's Law will continue to be valid, and neither the percentage of people who are employed nor the level of national income will shift.

(c) **Saving-Investment Equality in the Money Market:** According to the principles of classical economics, the money market is a particularly unique market that, if properly functioning, would provide parity between saving and investment, and thus, would guarantee full employment. They asserted that the interest rate was determined by the supply and demand for capital in the economy. The supply and demand for capital are both comprised of savings and investments taken together. The rate of interest that is considered "equilibrium" is established when the amount of money saved and invested is equal. Any disparity in the amount of money saved vs invested would be rectified by the interest rate. If people save more money than they invest, then interest rates will go down. As a consequence of this, increased investment will ensue, and the process will continue in this manner until parity is reached. Even the contrary is true in this case.

(d) **Price Flexibility:** Furthermore, according to traditional economists, any future decrease in total expenditure would be offset by a commensurate reduction in the price level even if the rate of interest did not match savings and investments. Even if the interest rate does not coincide with savings and investments, this is still true. To put it another way, if the cost drops to Rs. 25, Rs. 50, and Rs. 100 will each be able to buy two shirts at the previous price, whereas Rs. 25 will require Rs. Therefore, if households save more than businesses would invest, the subsequent decline in spending would not lead to a decrease in real output or real income, nor would it result in a reduction in the number of available jobs, given that product prices simultaneously decrease in the same proportion as well.

(e) **Wage Flexibility:** The conventional economists also believed that if consumer demand for commodities decreased, there would be a corresponding decrease in the demand for labour, which would lead to unemployment. But the wage rate would also drop, compelling jobless workers to accept lower compensation in order to keep their jobs. The process will continue until the wage rate is low enough to completely empty the labour market. The new, lower equilibrium pay rate will then be decided. As a result, involuntary unemployment was illogical in the traditional understanding.

6.2.3 Keynes Criticism of Classical Theory:

J.M. Keynes criticised the classical hypothesis for the following reasons:

1. According to Keynes, savings are unaffected by changes in interest rates and depend on national income. It is therefore impossible to balance savings and investments by changing interest rates. Say's Law will be rendered useless as a result.

2. The work market is far from perfect due to the presence of trade unions and government intervention in the form of minimum wage regulations. Salary flexibility is therefore unlikely. Wages are less pliable when they decline than when they rise. As a result, when S exceeds I, a reduction in demand will lead to a decrease in both employment and production.

3. Keynes argued that even if wages and prices were flexible, a free-market economy would not always be able to achieve automatic full employment.

6.3. Wage and price stickiness

Despite the fact that there are several schools of thought in macroeconomics, each one has been compelled to make an effort to explain the Phillips curve's existence or, in a similar vein, the reasons for wage and price stickiness. Since the solutions are not mutually exclusive, we shall briefly outline some of the more well-known hypotheses.

6.3.1. Imperfect Information—Market Clearing

Some economists have made the following attempts to explain the Phillips curve in a situation where markets are clear: Despite the entire flexibility of pay, adjustments to them take time due to short-term unrealistic expectations. Models by Milton Friedman and Edmund Phelps from the 1960s assume that workers would work harder when nominal wages rise as a result of rising prices because they mistakenly believe their zeal wage has grown. Therefore, until employees realise that the higher nominal compensation is just the result of a higher price level, an increase in the nominal wage is connected to a greater level of output and fewer jobs in the near run. According to these beliefs, the reason salaries don't adjust more quickly is because of employees' delayed reactions to or lack of awareness of price changes.

6.3.2 Coordination Problems

The coordination approach to the Phillips curve emphasises pricing changes made by businesses in response to changes in demand rather than pay fluctuations. Suppose the money stock increases. The final result will be a constant production with prices rising in lockstep with the money supply. The company that raised its price would, however, lose business to the other firms if no other firms increased their prices in proportion to the growth in the money stock. Naturally, the new equilibrium would be reached immediately if all firms raised their prices by the same amount. Although there is a boost in demand for goods at the existing prices as a result of the shift in the money supply, businesses in an economy are unable to join together to coordinate price increases, thus each will raise prices gradually.

Furthermore, coordination problems could help to explain why wages are sticky downward or why they do not fall immediately when aggregate demand falls. Employees who work for a firm that decreases compensation while other companies don't will eventually quit because they are unhappy. Due to the inability of firms to cooperate, salaries steadily decrease as individual companies reduce the minimal wages they pay their employees, maybe starting with the companies whose profits have been most adversely affected.

6.3.3 Efficiency Wages and Costs of Price Change

Efficiency pay theory focuses on the compensation as a recruitment tool for labour. The amount of labour that workers put in at work and how well the job pays in contrast to alternatives are connected. Businesses may choose to offer salaries that are higher than the market-clearing rate in order to motivate employees to put in extra effort and keep their excellent job.

While efficiency wage theory contributes to the understanding of why unemployment occurs, it does not by itself explain why average nominal earnings move slowly. Instead, it offers an explanation for why real wages vary slowly. The efficiency wage hypothesis, when coupled with this fact, can nevertheless result in significant stickiness in nominal wages even when the costs of resetting prices are quite low. This theory combines coordination problems with the stickiness of nominal wages to explain the stickiness of nominal wages.

6.3.4 Contracts and Long-term Relationships

We use the aforementioned theories as well as one crucial aspect to explain wage stickiness: the existence of long-term ties between employers and employees in the labour market. The majority of persons in the labour force want to stay in their existing jobs for a while. Working conditions, including the salary, are occasionally renegotiated since it is expensive to do so on a regular basis. Even in circumstances when the compensation is supposed to be set by market conditions, it is expensive to obtain the relevant information regarding alternative pay. The majority of the time, salary is reviewed by both employers and employees once each year, at most.

Salaries are often calculated in nominal terms in countries with low inflation rates. As a consequence, it is agreed that over the next three months or for a full year, the employer would pay the employee a specific sum per hour or per month. The bulk of formal union employment contracts are two or three years long, during which time they may also establish minimal remuneration. The fact that employment contracts commonly include different compensation rates for extra hours implies that the pay rate paid by employers is greater when more hours are worked. This is one of the reasons why the WN curve in Figure 6.9 has a positive slope.

Employers and workers may have made a formal or informal agreement on the salary schedule that is to be paid to existing employees at any moment. Depending on the type of job, basic pay will be based on the weekly total of hours worked and may increase for overtime. Thus, the corporation always decides the degree of employment.

Examine now how wages alter when the employment market changes and enterprises increase their operating hours. In the near run, wages rise following the WN curve. Given the increasing demand, workers might anticipate a basic wage increase during the ensuing round of labour talks. But it will take some time until all salaries are renegotiated. Furthermore, not all remuneration is discussed at once. The dates for establishing salaries are instead spread apart so that they coincide. Assume that pay for half the workforce are decided in January and for the other half in July. Let's assume that the money stock rises in September. Since wages won't change until three months after the money stock changes, prices will shift gradually. Additionally, when it comes time to renegotiate half of the contracts in January, both the employers and the employees are aware that other earnings won't alter for the ensuing six months.

To the extent that the economy finds long-term equilibrium, workers do not try to increase their base wage. If they did, their salary would be significantly more than other wages during the subsequent six months, and companies would pick to recruit those workers whose salaries have not yet grown. The January wage-setting workers run the danger of losing their employment if the renegotiated compensation is too high. As a result, just a small portion of the equilibrium wage adjustment is made.

The other half of the wages are not driven all the way to the equilibrium level when it comes time to reset them in July since the January wages would then be significantly lower. As a result, the July earnings are greater than the January wages, but they still fall short of fully achieving the minimum level required for full employment.

As salaries advance one another and are renegotiated one at a time in this process of staggered price adjustment, the supply curve increases from period to period. The location of the aggregate supply curve in each period will depend on where it was in the preceding period since each unit that is renegotiating pay must consider the level of its salary relative to the wages that are not being reset. The level of the earnings that are not being reset is also reflected in the wage rate from the prior pay period.

Businesses will also modify their pricing when salaries (and therefore, enterprises' expenses) change during the adjustment process. The wage and price adjustment procedure is repeated once the economy has returned to full-employment equilibrium with the same real balances. The adjustment procedure in real life is more difficult since salaries are not reset consistently, as in our January-July example, and because both salary and price variations are significant. The example from January to July, however, demonstrates how modifications are done.

This portrayal of a steady rise in prices and salaries raises at least two crucial inquiries. First, given that economic challenges are clear-cut and understandable, why don't companies and employees boost wages more frequently? If they did, they may be able to adjust wages in order to maintain a fully employed work force. A corpus of research emphasises the possibility that even negligible expenses connected with resetting wages and prices might slow down adjustment processes. It is challenging to coordinate wage and price modifications such that wages and prices swiftly return to equilibrium in a large economy with multiple dynamics affecting supply and demand in distinct areas.

Second, in times of high unemployment, why don't firms and jobless workers combine to negotiate wage reductions that result in jobs for the unemployed? The main cause of this—that these procedures are bad for employees' morale and, hence, their output—is addressed by the efficiency pay hypothesis.

In conclusion, a combination of wages that are fixed for a certain length of time and pay changes that are staggered results in the gradual wage, price, and production adjustment we observe in the real world. This explains the increasing vertical shift of the short-run aggregate supply curve.

6.4. From Phillip's curve to the aggregate supply curve

We may proceed back to the aggregate supply curve now that we have the Phillips curve. The derivation involves four stages. To begin, we translate output into employment. Second, we connect the fees that companies charge to their costs. The Phillips curve, which connects incomes to employment, is our third method of profit. Fourth, we combine the three components to produce an upward-sloping aggregate supply curve.

6.5. Long-run aggregate supply curve

An example of the long-term link between actual output and price level, with ceteris paribus applied to all other variables affecting aggregate supply. The long-run aggregate supply curve, often known as the LRAS, is one of two curves that graphically depict the supply-side of the aggregate market. The other is the short-term aggregate supply curve. The demand-side of the whole market is occupied by the aggregate demand curve. The vertical long-run aggregate supply curve captures the independent link between long-term real production and price level.

The long-run aggregate supply curve illustrates the lack of a cause-and-effect relationship between real production and price level. As the price level rises, real production remains constant at the moment of full employment. At full employment, real production remains constant while the price level falls. Because prices are adjustable, the same amount of real output is created at every price level.

The interaction between the aggregate supply and demand curves over the long run as well as the aggregate supply curve over the short term is the fundamental working principle of the aggregate market (or AS-AD) analysis. Then, utilising this theory, macroeconomic phenomena are clarified and comprehended, including business cycles, inflation, unemployment, and stabilisation measures.

Figure 6.5. The long run aggregate supply curve

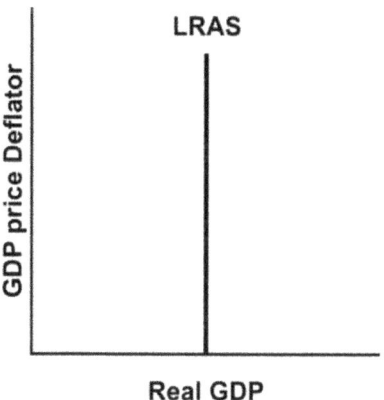

- To begin with, the horizontal axis is used to measure real production, while the vertical axis is used to monitor price level. While real GDP is used to quantify actual production, the GDP price deflator is often used to assess pricing levels.

- The aggregate supply curve is vertical over the long run. The commercial sector sells the same amount of the entire actual production at higher and lower price points. The total real production at this steady state level is at full employment.

- Third, the price level and total actual production are the only two factors that can change while this curve is being created. It is assumed that nothing else alters that would, over time, have an effect on aggregate supply. These additional factors are ceteris paribus components that, like market supply, are aggregate supply determinants.

- Fourth, this long-run aggregate supply curve captures the link between price level and the flow of actual output over a certain time period. However, depending on the specific aggregate market study, the time period might be shorter (a few months) or longer (a few years). In reality, if the time horizon is too short, the long-run aggregate supply curve could not be meaningful.

6.6. Questions

1. Critically examine Classical Theory of Employment.
2. Explain in detail why wages are sticky.
3. Explain long run Aggregate Supply Curve.

Chapter 7

Inflation and Money

7.1. Introduction

Monetary inflation is a persistent increase in a country's money supply. Price inflation, which is often the result, refers to an increase in the average level of products and service costs. The term "inflation" was first largely used to refer to monetary inflation; nowadays, it is more usually used to refer to price inflation.

Changes in the economy's money supply and demand are mostly brought about by inflation. Over time, rising prices for goods and services is referred to as inflation. There will be an excess of money chasing a constrained supply of goods and services, which will result in higher prices, if the quantity of money in an economy grows faster than the rise in production. Because customers have more money to spend, inflation is driven by demand, and businesses can raise prices to satisfy this demand.

A decline in the supply of products and services in comparison to demand can cause inflation, which results in increased prices. For instance, if a natural catastrophe or supply shock restricts the availability of a key commodity, the price of that commodity and the products and services that depend on it may increase.

To regulate the money supply and lower inflation, central banks employ monetary policy tools include modifying interest rates, reserve requirements, and open market operations. The central bank can lower the quantity of money in circulation and control demand-driven inflation by raising interest rates. As an alternative, the central bank can boost economic activity and expand the money supply to boost demand and counteract supply-driven inflation.

A crucial indication of economic development, income equality, and social wellbeing is inflation. High and unpredictably fluctuating inflation can diminish people's and companies' purchasing power, discourage investment, and sow economic instability. In an inflationary environment, central banks and decision-makers must carefully control the money supply in the economy to preserve price stability and advance sustainable economic growth.

Although economists usually agree on the supply and demand of money as well as the prices of goods and services expressed in monetary terms, they disagree on the exact process and connection between price inflation and monetary inflation. The system is complex, and there is considerable discussion over important issues like how to measure the monetary base, how much factors like the velocity of money affect the relationship, and what the best monetary policy should be. There is unanimity about the importance and responsibility of central banks and monetary authorities in affecting inflation. Keynesian economists are in favour of monetary policies aimed at balancing the ups and downs of the business cycle. Most central banks currently follow this standard, altering monetary policy in response to inflation and unemployment. Monetarists favour either a continuous rise in the amount of money in circulation or the targeting of inflation.

7.2. The Phillip's curve

The essential principle of the Phillips Curve is that inflation and unemployment must be short-term trade-offs. When we examine the statistics for unemployment and inflation in Britain over the previous fifteen years, we will notice that the nature of the trade-off has changed for the economy and other elements as well. However, monetarist economists have persistently criticised the original Phillips Curve.

The Phillips Curve's central idea: economic trade-offs: In 1958, Phillips, who gave the Phillips Curve its name, plotted 95 years' worth of data in the UK to compare unemployment and wage inflation. It seemed to suggest a short-term trade-off between unemployment and inflation. This was based on a rather straightforward idea. While allowing unemployment to increase may be the only method to lower inflation, falling unemployment may lead to rising inflation. If the government wanted to decrease the unemployment rate, it might enhance aggregate demand, but even while this could immediately increase employment, it may also have inflationary consequences on the labour and product markets. In order to fully grasp this trade-off, it is necessary to consider the possible consequences of inflation on the labour and product markets that may arise from an increase in national income, production, and employment.

The labour market: Labour shortages may arise in areas where skilled employees are in short supply when the unemployment rate falls. Due to the increased pressure on wages to rise and the fact that salaries sometimes make up a significant percentage of overall expenses, prices may rise as a result of firms passing these costs along to their customers.

Further factor markets Price increases may also be caused by increased demand for finished goods like steel, glass, and concrete as well as for raw resources like copper and oil. While the economy is booming, there is an increase in demand for certain components and raw materials.

Increased supply and demand in the merchandise market put pressure on scarce resources, which might lead to suppliers raising prices to boost profit margins. Price hikes are more likely to occur when there is a shortage of supply and an abundance of demand. (Or an increase in the production gap)

7.2.1 Explaining the Phillips Curve concept using AD-AS and the output gap

Let's consider the trade-off explanation that makes use of AD-AS analysis and the output gap concept. The LRAS curve is shown as vertical in the accompanying graphic on the assumption that the level of prices has no impact on an economy's long-term productivity.

We see an outward movement of the AD curve, which, for example, results from a sharp rise in consumer spending, elevates the equilibrium level of national production to Y2 above potential GDP Yfc. These have the effect of creating a positive production gap, which is thought to be the primary cause of the rise in inflationary pressure described above. The excessive demand in the product and factor markets results in high manufacturing costs, which cause the short-term aggregate supply to go from SRAS1 to SRAS2. The supply reduction causes the economy to produce at its potential level, albeit at a higher price level.

Fig 7.2

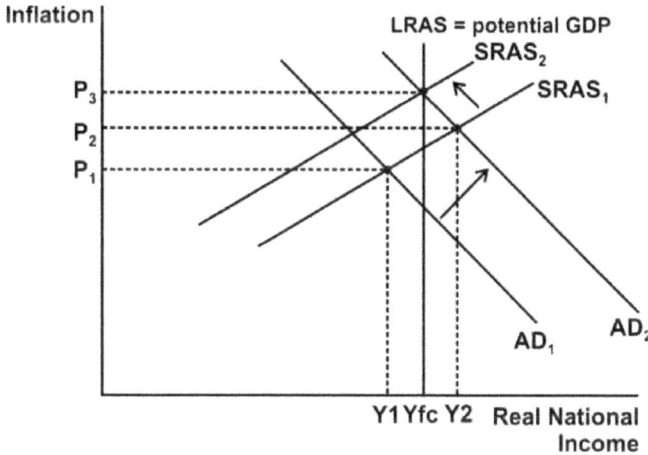

As a result, this could help to clarify the Phillips Curve idea. We may also use a non-linear SRAS curve in a graphic to demonstrate the concept. The following diagram shows the initial short-run Phillips Curve and the trade-off between inflation and unemployment:

Figure 7.3

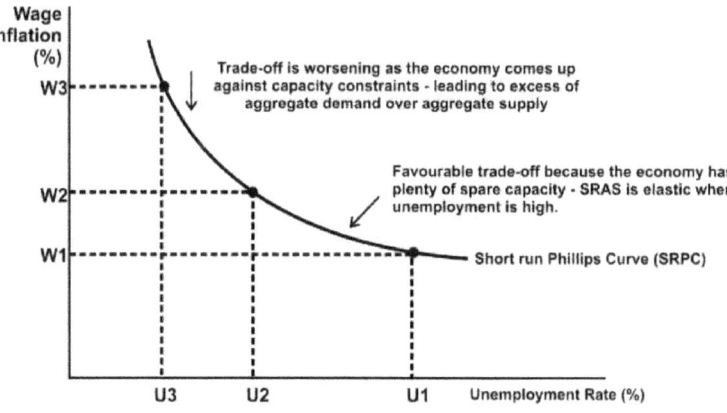

7.3. The nairu : the non-accelerating-inflation rate of unemployment.

Milton Friedman, who criticised the fundamental presumptions of the original Phillips Curve in a 1968 speech to the American Economic Association, was the first to put out the NAIRU notion. It has been enhanced by economists in the US and the UK. The NAIRU concept was developed in the UK with assistance from Sir Richard Layard and Prof. Stephen Nickell at the LSE.

As a member of the Monetary Policy Committee, Nickell presently takes part in the decision-making process that determines interest rates.

The NAIRU is the rate of unemployment when the rate of wage inflation is constant.

The NAIRU bases its argument on the idea that there is imperfect competition in the job market and that some workers can engage in collective bargaining with their employers because they belong to a union. Additionally, some companies have a limited amount of monopolistic power when purchasing labour inputs.

According to NAIRU supporters, a bargaining process between employers and employees leads to the equilibrium level of unemployment. Employees under this notion are thinking about a goal actual salary. This target real wage is affected by the unemployment rate since it is assumed that workers would demand greater pay as the unemployment rate declines. Workers will attempt to bargain for a larger share of rising earnings while the economy is experiencing a cyclical upturn.

In part, whether or not a firm will be able to reach that target real wage during pay discussions depends on its capacity to apply a markup to cost in the product markets in which it competes. In highly competitive markets with many suppliers competing, one would predict smaller mark-ups (i.e., lower profit margins). Employees may decide to bargain for a bigger share of the "producer surpluses" in markets with dominant suppliers because the cost markup is often substantially higher in these areas.

Theoretically, if real unemployment falls below the NAIRU, the balance of power in the labour market tends to move away from employers and towards employees. Pay agreements may advance and average incomes may rise as a consequence, which would benefit the economy. increased wage inflation will often lead to increased cost-push inflationary pressure.

7.3.1 The expectations-augmented Phillips Curve

The first Phillips Curve theory was fiercely contested by the Monetarist school, which included American economist Milton Friedman. In the short term, Friedman recognised the Phillips Curve's existence, but said that in the long run, there was no trade-off between unemployment and inflation and that the Phillips Curve was vertical.

He asserted that a precise anticipated inflation rate was used to generate each short-run Phillips Curve. Therefore, if inflation rose as a result of a big monetary expansion and this had the effect of rising inflationary expectations, the short term Phillips Curve would shift upward.

Initiatives to boost AD in an effort to speed up growth and reduce unemployment, in line with the monetarist viewpoint, only temporarily affect employment. Friedman argued that a government could not maintain unemployment below the NAIRU since doing so would cause inflation to increase, which in turn would ultimately cause unemployment to increase again while simultaneously rising inflation expectations.

Friedman popularised the idea of adaptive expectations, which holds that if individuals notice and experience rising inflation in their everyday lives, they would anticipate higher average inflation rates in the future. Workers (or the unions that represent them) may then take into consideration these changing expectations when negotiating their compensation. Prices often reflect changes in earnings. A surge in price inflation may lead to more salary claims, more labour costs, and finally higher prices for the goods and services we need and want to buy.

The accompanying diagram, where SPRC2 has higher inflation forecasts, illustrates this. As a result, in order to keep inflation at a specific target level, it may be required to raise the unemployment rate.

Figure 8.3

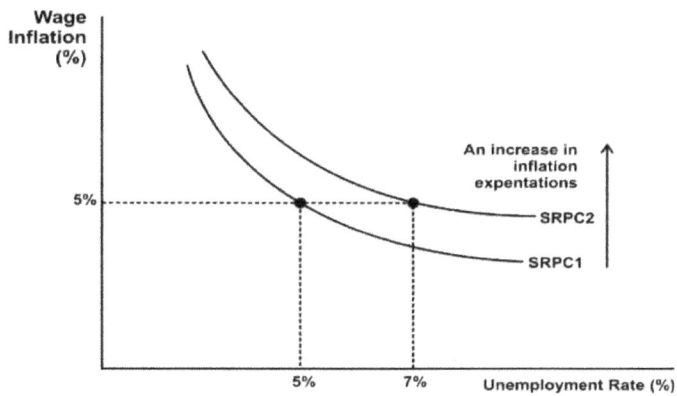

The Phillips Curve indicates that it is doubtful that government measures to reduce unemployment below the natural rate of unemployment by raising aggregate demand would be successful over the long run. Simply put, the result is more inflation and higher inflation expectations. The monetarist school holds that the best approach to lower inflation is to strictly regulate credit and money. Credible inflation control methods that successfully decrease inflation expectations can cause the Phillips Curve to move downward.

7.4. The long run Philips curve

Although the long run Phillips Curve is typically depicted as vertical, it can tilt inwards over time.

Figure 7.4

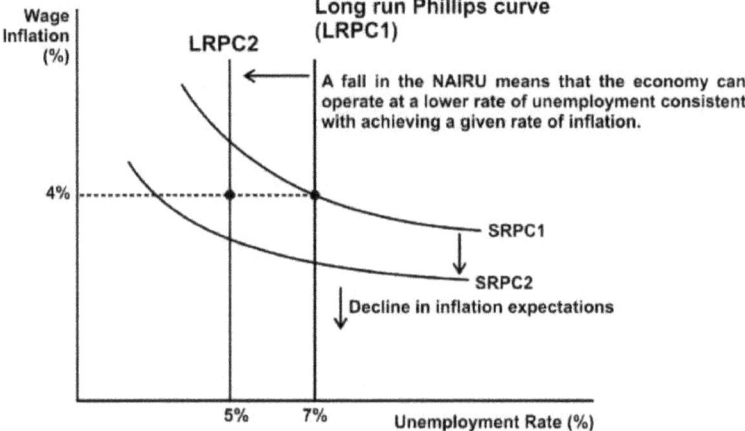

The long-run Phillips Curve may shift inward as a result of supply-side economic changes, particularly if the natural rate of unemployment decreases. For instance, labour market changes may be successful in reducing structural and frictional unemployment, maybe as a consequence of stronger job search incentives or advancements in the human capital of the workforce that boost occupational mobility of employees.

7.5. Economics policies to control inflation

The management of inflation is currently one of the primary objectives of government economic policy in many countries. Effective efforts to contain inflation must concentrate on the underlying causes of inflation in the economy. For instance, government policy should attempt to reduce aggregate demand if it is the main contributing element and excessive demand for products and services. If cost-push inflation is the fundamental problem, then the solution is to lower production costs.

7.5.1 Monetary Policy

Monetary policy may impede demand growth by increasing interest rates and limiting the supply of real money. For example, because of the economy's unrestrained expansion in the late 1980s, interest rates rose to 13% and contributed to the recession that began in the early 1990s. The following are the effects of rising interest rates:

By discouraging borrowing by both individuals and corporations, rising interest rates lower aggregate demand in three different ways.

- The potential cost of spending has grown, which has accelerated saving; the rise in mortgage interest payments has decreased homeowners' real "effective" disposable income and purchasing power. A decrease in demand for homes will result from rising mortgage rates.
- Rising borrowing prices may cause a decrease in business investment. Aggregate demand will decrease as a result of a few projects that were previously predicted to lose money.
- Another strategy for preventing price inflation is to raise interest rates. In order to reduce the demand for loans and, as a result, the expansion of broad money, real interest rates should rise.

7.5.2 Fiscal Policy

• Increased direct taxes (causing a fall in disposable income)

• Less government spending;

• A decrease in the amount borrowed by the government sector each year (PSNCR)

These fiscal changes will result in slower economic growth and more unemployment, as well as a rise in income leakage from the circular flow and a fall in injections into it. Additionally, they will reduce demand-pull inflation.

7.5.3 An appreciation of the exchange rate

The cost of Indian exports rises due to a higher rupee, which should reduce global demand and export volume. It also provides Indian companies a motive to cut costs in order to compete internationally. A stronger Rupee reduces import prices. It helps firms reduce costs by lowering the cost of the raw materials and components they utilise.

Two methods to raise the currency rate's value include raising interest rates and central banks buying Indian rupees by intervening in the foreign exchange markets.

7.5.4 Directly affecting wages and incomes

By regulating the amount of salary growth, incomes policies (or outright pay limits) may be able to reduce cost inflation. The government still tries to limit wage growth even though it hasn't used a method like this since the late 1970s by regulating public sector pay increases and setting cash limitations for employee compensation.

To persuade employers and employees to be reasonable in pay negotiations, the government may utilise moral persuasion in the private sector. This seldom suffices on its own. Wage inflation often decreases when the economy is on the cusp of a recession and unemployment is starting to rise. This leads to more work instability, and some employees may trade some employment protection for claims of lower pay.

Limitations on wages and prices have proved helpful during wartime in addition to rationing. However, their applicability in other situations is significantly more inconsistent. Richard Nixon's imposition of wage and price limitations in 1972 is a famous instance of its abuse. More useful examples are the Wassenaar Agreement in the Netherlands and the Prices and Incomes Accord in Australia.

Wage and price controls are typically seen as a temporary and exceptional instrument that only functions when used in conjunction with other initiatives targeted at lowering the underlying causes of inflation prior to the wage and price control regime, such as winning the ongoing war. They typically have negative effects because they provide false signals to the market. Artificially low prices typically cause rationing, shortages, and a reduction in future investment, all of which contribute to an ongoing cycle of shortages. When a commodity or service is underpriced, overconsumption is said to occur, according to traditional economic theory. For instance, if the official price of bread is set too low, there won't be enough bread available at the official price and the market won't be investing enough in bread production to satisfy future requirements, which will make the problem worse over time.

In order to prevent inflation during a recession, temporary measures may be employed. In addition to eliminating the types of distortions that temporary regulations cause while demand is high, this would lessen the need to increase unemployment. Economists frequently recommend price liberalisation over price limits because they think the economy will correct itself and stop participating in wasteful spending. The labour or resource prices that were driving inflation will fall along with total economic output as a result of the decreased activity.

Redistribution of productive capacity typically results in a severe recession, which makes it extremely unpopular with those whose livelihoods are destroyed.

7.6. Long-term policies to control inflation

7.6.1 Labour market reforms

Because of the decline in the power of unions, the rise of temporary and part-time labour, and flexible work hours, the labour market has grown more adaptable. Inflationary pressure may be reduced if firms are able to keep their employment costs in check.

It's undeniable that the economy has not lately seen the rise in wage inflation that is frequently brought on by several years of steady economic development and falling inflation. One explanation is that a flexible labour market and increasing job insecurity have tipped the power scales in favour of businesses.

7.6.2 Supply-side reforms

If more can be produced for a lower cost per unit, the economy can develop continuously without experiencing inflation. Most often, a key long-term objective of state economic policy is to increase total supply. The graph below illustrates the benefits of an outward shift in the aggregate supply curve over the long term. Real national income increases until it reaches its equilibrium level, while the average price level mostly remains constant.

Figure 8.5

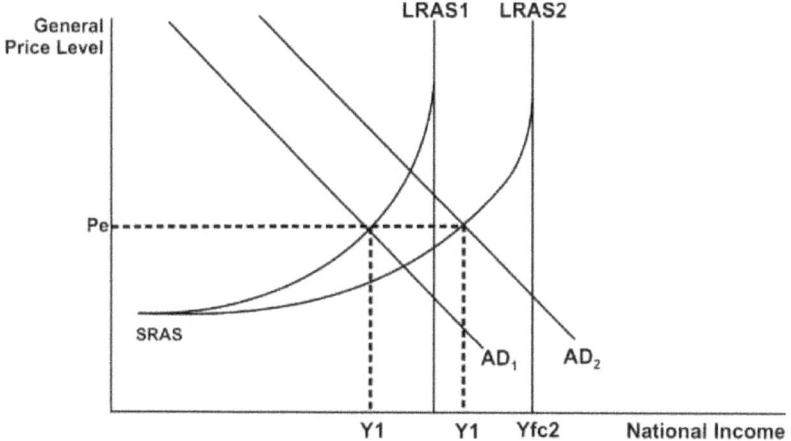

Supply side reforms seek to increase the economy's long-term productive potential by increasing the trend rate of development of labour and capital productivity. Numerous supply-side policies have been put into place in the Indian economy recently.

Gains in productivity help to manage unit labour costs, a major factor in cost-push inflation, which lessens the pressure on manufacturers to raise their prices.

In order to sustain aggregate demand management over time (through fiscal and monetary policy), the government must also seek to strengthen the supply side of the economy. The credibility of an inflation control programme may frequently be increased by include inflation objectives.

7.6.3 Cost-of-living allowance

The actual buying power of fixed payments will decrease if they aren't changed for inflation to retain their true values. A cost-of-living index, often the consumer price index, is frequently linked to employment agreements, pension payments, and government benefits (like social security).

A cost-of-living allowance (COLA) is added to salaries to reflect changes in a cost-of-living index. Salary adjustments are frequently conducted once a year in countries with minimal inflation. A hyperinflation increases the frequency of modifications. If an employee moves, they could also be compensated according to a region-specific cost-of-living index.

Annual escalation provisions in employment contracts are sometimes used to describe past or future percentage pay increases that are unconnected to any index. These negotiated pay increases are sometimes referred to as cost-of-living adjustments or cost-of-living raises due to their similarity to pay increases related to externally established indices. Many economists and pay experts consider the idea of predetermined future "cost of living increases" to be misleading for two reasons: (1) For the majority of recent periods in the industrialised world, average wages have grown faster than most cost-of-living indexes, reflecting the influence of rising productivity and worker bargaining power rather than just living costs; and (2) the majority of cost-of-living indexes are not forward-looking, but rather compare current prices with those in the past.

7.6.4 Problems with forecasting inflation

Inflation cannot be predicted precisely. The total inflation rate is the outcome of millions of price decisions made by both large and small businesses. The retail price index calculation is quite rigorous, yet it is nevertheless prone to mistakes and omissions. Furthermore, predicting is exceedingly challenging due to the complexity of the inflation process, even when the economy's inflationary conditions appear to be benign.

Projections may be affected by foreign economic shocks. Examples of shocks that have a large impact on the economy include a rapid rise in global oil prices (an inflationary shock) or a sudden fall in the value of the world's equities (a deflationary shock). The exchange rate may cause changes in the cost of imported goods and services.

7.7. Fisher's equation

One of the most contentious policy discussions that occurred in the postwar era was built on the quantity theory, or at least a significant portion of it. In order to help smooth out the cyclical ups and downs that we have referred to as the business cycle back then and continue to refer to it now, a huge number of entrepreneurs, economists, and government officials felt that monetary policy should be chosen to micromanage or fine-tune the economy. This idea is still widely held today.

The Fisher equation is a theory used in economics to characterise the connection between nominal and real interest rates while accounting for the effects of inflation. The equation shows that the nominal interest rate is equal to the sum of the real interest rate and inflation, and this amount is equal to the nominal interest rate.

When investors or lenders want more compensation to make up for losses in purchasing power brought on by high inflation rates, the Fisher equation is typically used.

Figure 7.7. The Fisher Equation

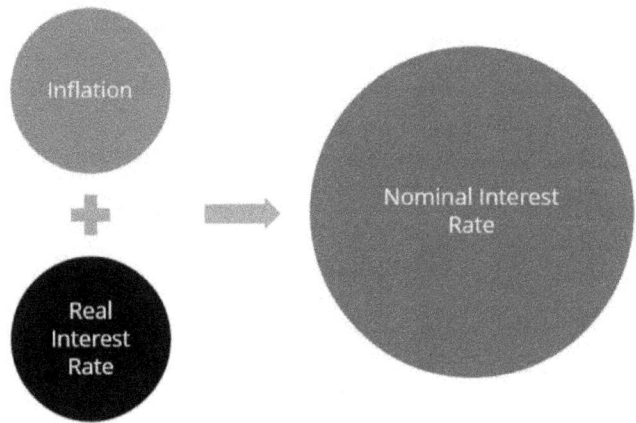

The idea is heavily utilised in the practises of the domains of finance and economics. It is used rather frequently for calculating investment returns or generating predictions about the behaviour of nominal and real interest rates. The situation where an investor seeks to determine the true (real) interest rate earned on an investment after accounting for the influence that inflation has had is an excellent example of this.

One of the remarkable results of the Fisher equation has to do with monetary policy. The equation shows that both inflation and nominal interest rate changes are influenced by changes in monetary policy, and that both changes happen simultaneously and in the same direction. The real interest rate, on the other hand, appears to be minimally affected by monetary policy, according to the available information.

Irving Fisher, a US economist, came up with the equation.

(1 + i) = (1 + r) (1 + À)

Where:

i – the nominal interest rate

r – the real interest rate

π – the inflation rate

7.8. Quantity theory of money

The monetarist theory of inflation is based on the Quantity Theory of Money, or MV = PT, where M is the Money Supply, V is the Velocity of Circulation, P is the Price Level, and T is Transactions or Output. Because monetarists think that real forces, including the economy's productive capacity, ultimately influence V and T, there is a clear relationship between the growth of the money supply and inflation.

We examine the several channels through which an abundance of money might cause inflation below. Additionally, customers can make direct purchases of products and services using their leftover balances. As a result, rising aggregate demand has a direct effect on inflation. Additional increases in unit labour costs and money pay will be brought on by higher demands for goods and services. The inelasticity of the economy's total supply has an increasing effect on inflation.

The rise in demand for goods and services may lead to an increase in imports. Although this leakage from the domestic economy reduces the money supply, it increases the quantity of money accessible on the foreign currency market, which lowers the exchange rate. It could lead to inflation that is imported.

The Fisher equation in financial mathematics and economics estimates the relationship between nominal and real interest rates under inflation. It is named after Irving Fisher, a writer well known for his works on the theory of interest. The Fisher equation is frequently applied in finance to determine the YTM of bonds or the IRR of investments. In economics, this equation is used to predict how nominal and real interest rates will behave. Here is the Fisher equation: Assume that r stands for real interest rate, i for nominal interest rate, and n for inflation rate. (Please take notice that economists frequently use the Greek letter 'n' for the constant 3.14159 when referring to inflation rates.)

This is an approximate linear approximation even though it is commonly represented as an equality:

$i = r + n$

The Fisher equation can be applied to ex-ante (before) and ex-post (after) studies. It can be used ex-post to communicate the actual purchasing power of a loan:

$r = i - n$

When rearranged into an expectation-augmented Fisher equation and given a desired real rate of return and an anticipated rate of inflation over the course of a loan, it can be used ex ante to determine the nominal rate that should be charged for the loan. Despite Fisher's proposal for a more precise approximation, which is provided below, this equation already existed. The approximate equation is produced by the precise one:

$1 + i = (1 + r)(1 + n)$

7.8.1 Derivation of the equation

Even though time subscripts are occasionally dropped, the Fisher equation is based on the relationship between nominal and real interest rates through inflation and the percentage change in the price level between two time periods. So let's imagine that someone buys a $1 bond at that specific interest rate in period t. During time t+1, the buyer will receive (1 + it) dollars upon redemption. The real value of the bond's proceeds, however, would be larger if the price level rose between period t and period t+1.

$(1 + rt + 1) = (1 + it) / (1 + n\,t + 1)$

The nominal interest rate can be calculated from this point.

$1 + it = (1 + rt + 1)(1 + n\,t + 1)$ (1)

In expanded form, the equation stated in (1) becomes:

$1 + it = 1 + rt + 1 + n\,t + 1 + rt + 1n\,t + 1$

$it = rt + 1 + n\,t + 1 + rt + 1n_t + 1$

The final estimate may be obtained by deleting rt + 1n t + 1 because it is much larger than rt + 1 + n t + 1. This presumption states that real interest rates and inflation rates are both very low (perhaps a few percent range, depending on the application).Applications of the Fisher's Equation 7.8.2

The Fisher equation has important implications for the trading of inflation-indexed bonds since changes in coupon payments depend on changes in break-even inflation, real interest rates, and nominal interest rates.

7.8.3 Fisher hypothesis

The Fisher hypothesis or Fisher parity in economics refers to Irving Fisher's assertion that the real interest rate is independent of monetary measurements, notably the nominal interest rate. The Fisher equation is

$rr = rn - n^e$.

In other terms, the real interest rate (rr) is equal to the nominal interest rate (rn) minus projected inflation. (n). In this case, all rates are compounded continuously. For simple rates, the Fisher equation looks like this:

Rn must rise as ne rises if rr is assumed to remain constant. Fisher's Effect To take into account predicted inflation, the nominal interest rate is multiplied by one.

Understanding the link between money, inflation, and interest rates requires an understanding of both the nominal interest rate and the real interest rate. The nominal interest rate is the figure you hear mentioned at your bank. For instance, a savings account's nominal interest rate will show how rapidly the balance will grow over time. By accounting for the effects of inflation on the nominal rate, the real interest rate provides information on how rapidly the buying power of your savings account will grow over time. The real interest rate may be calculated using a straightforward method by subtracting the nominal interest rate from the expected inflation rate. (Note that when considering compounding savings, this estimate is foolish.)

Real interest rate is the nominal interest rate less expected inflation.

Nominal Interest Rate = Real Interest Rate + Expected Inflation Rate

If inflation increased from a constant level, let's say 4%/yr, to a constant level, let's say 8%/yr, the interest rate on such currency would eventually catch up to the higher inflation, growing by 4 points a year from their beginning level. These modifications have no impact on the real return on that investment. The Fisher Effect is evidence that the country's relative prices will not be affected by long-term changes in the money supply.

According to the International Fisher Effect, national nominal interest rates alone will decide the direction of the global exchange rate, regardless of inflation. (However, if inflation is internationally harmonised, unequal real rates will result in the same exchange rate drift.)

7.9. Inflation tax

The value loss sustained by owners of cash, fixed-rate bonds, and fixed-income (income that is not tied to inflation) as a result of the effects of inflation is referred to as the "inflation tax." The popular metaphor for this monetary loss of value is the loss of buying power. It could be more appropriately referred to as a wealth transfer rather than a tax because many individuals, including creditors, owners of actual assets, and certain investors, may benefit at the same time. Because they keep a larger portion of their income in cash, are much less likely to receive newly created money before the market has adjusted with inflated prices, are more likely to have fixed incomes, wages, or pensions, and lack the ability to transfer assets abroad to avoid domestic inflation, many economists believe that the lower and middle classes are more affected by inflation than the wealthy. Some contend that inflation functions as a regressive, non-linear consumption tax. However, individuals with existing debt with fixed interest rates, such as mortgages and school loans, stand to gain from inflation.

By encouraging exports with a more cost-effective currency and lowering imports, it can improve the nation's trade balance. The "tax" also unfairly disadvantages international investors that hold fixed income debt with inflated currency as the par value. It's critical to keep in mind that this "tax" on creditors also benefits borrowers by reducing their loan burden through a transfer. A "tax" on inflation that redistributes money to those who are more willing to spend it can help to further increase real (inflation adjusted) economic growth. (Outside of its favourable effects on commerce). It can possibly speed up new purchases because maintaining currency costs money due to inflation. Inflation can help troubled real estate markets by increasing liquidity since it would push nominal asset prices back up above loan values. This improved LTV has the potential to improve the efficiency of the labour markets by enabling people to sell their houses and relocate in quest of better work opportunities. This is one method that a "inflation tax" might increase employment and real (inflation-adjusted) economic growth. In light of this, a very restrictive monetary policy that seeks to reduce inflation even at the price of actual (inflation adjusted) economic progress and jobs may be referred to as a "stagnation tax."

7.9.1 How it happens?

When central banks print money and provide credit, there is more money available in the economy. This is occasionally done in reaction to poor economic circumstances. It is generally acknowledged that inflation occurs from a gradual increase in the money supply. Some have argued that increasing the money supply and requiring money owners to pay an inflation tax actually constitute taxation. If annual inflation in the United States is 5%, a dollar will purchase $1 worth of goods and services this year, but $1.05 will be required to purchase the same goods or services the following year; ceteris paribus, this has the same effect as a 5% annual tax on cash holdings.

Governments almost always have net debt. (That is, most of the time a government owes more money than others owe to it). Inflation increases tax income while simultaneously decreasing the relative value of earlier borrowing. Therefore, it follows that a government can lower the debt-to-revenue ratio by implementing inflationary measures. The debt papers will be affected by inflation and lose value, making them less appealing to creditors, up until the government runs out of interested purchasers, if the government continues to sell debt by borrowing money in return for debt papers. Not all inflation taxes include debt creation. Just printing currency will increase liquidity and might result in inflationary pressures. The public will then be taxed on income and consumer expenditure to raise the additional funds. However, societal problems are frequently brought on by inflation. (For instance, when income growth lags price growth).

7.9.2 "Tax on the inflation tax" Even if the term "inflation tax" is not meant to indicate it, the tax on interest and investment "income," which is measured against the nominal interest rate or nominal profits, has a commensurate impact.

For instance, if someone buys a bond with a nominal interest rate of 6% and an inflation rate of 4%, the "real" interest rate is 1.92%.

In contrast, if they pay 1.5% in taxes, or 25% of the 6% interest "income," this may be seen as consisting of a tax on actual income (0.5%) plus an inflation tax (1.0%). The same reasoning also applies to non-inflation adjusted capital "gains" taxes. Anyhow, this "tax on the inflation tax" is essentially equivalent to a wealth tax that is determined by multiplying the nominal tax rate by the inflation rate (in the example above, 25% of 4% inflation is 1.0%). This "property tax" may be imposed on non-financial assets in addition to money that earns interest. Money is consequently liable to both the inflation tax and the tax on the inflation tax, in contrast to other assets, which are only subject to the inflation tax but are also subject to nominal profit or gain taxes.

Even inflation-indexed bonds incur inflation risk as a result of this levy as the inflation compensation is taxed.

7.9.3 Negative interest rates

A real interest rate that is negative means that interest rates are greater than inflation. For example, if the federal funds rate is 2% and inflation is 10%, the borrower would profit $7.27 on every dollar borrowed. Investment and business cycles may result from the borrower making a net profit by returning the principle with inflated (devalued) currency.

Why is the increased use of the "inflation tax" by governments so terrible? As long as it is utilised in combination with an inflation-targeting Fed, all the negative effects of inflation can be controlled. That is, as long as the Fed establishes a target inflation rate (let's say, 15%) and then uses open market strategies to bring inflation into line by taking into account the additional money, there won't be any unexpected inflation and, hence, no inflation cost.

7.9.4 Advantages of Inflation Tax

The benefits of the inflation tax are numerous, including: 1) Painless and free "collection." 2. Progression (those who have amassed the most wealth pay the most.)It's a thought-provoking proposal.

6. The inflation tax is unpleasant. Even if inflation is predictable and consistent, it nonetheless has a number of unfavourable effects. Included in these are the "shoe leather" costs linked to reduced actual money balances, higher menu prices, artificial relative pricing fluctuations, and tax distortions brought on by insufficiently indexed tax legislation. More information on them is provided in the textbook.

7. The inflation tax is probably not as progressive as one may initially think, contrary to popular belief. Only non-interest-bearing assets, such as cash, are subject to this tax; other assets are not. Most of the money that the affluent people possess may be preserved in methods that are immune from the inflation tax. (One exception is the wealthy in the shadow economy; the inflation tax may be especially harsh on criminals.)

8. The tax on inflation would only bring in a little amount of money. Here is a ballpark figure. The current size of the money supply is about $800 billion. A 15% inflation rate would therefore produce up to $120 billion yearly, or around 1% of GDP. That serves as a ceiling on tax revenue since the tax base would decrease as inflation rose and less money would be needed. (This is an example of a typical "Laffer curve" defence of the inflation tax.)

9. For unknown reasons, high inflation frequently causes irregular inflation. Economic theory predicts that an inflation rate of 15% will be steady and predictable, however this is rarely or never observed in practise. If we take

this empirical regularity as a limitation, the choice of high inflation requires the choice of fluctuating inflation, which increases uncertainty.

7.10. Questions

1. 'Short term trade-off between unemployment and inflation'
Explain the statement with reference to Phillips curve.
2. Explain the Expectations augmented Phillips curve.
3. Discuss in detail the Fisher's explanation of money.
4. What do you understand by Inflation Tax?

Chapter 8

Budget constraint: Money and Debt Financing of Budget Deficits

8.1. Introduction

Budget restrictions relate to the maximum quantity of goods and services that a person or organisation may purchase in light of their income and the cost of those same goods and services.

The government's budgetary restraint is defined as follows in macroeconomics:

Tax income plus borrowing equals government spending.

If the government's spending exceeds its tax receipts, it will need to borrow to make up the shortfall. This can eventually result in debt buildup, which has an impact on the economy's long-term development and stability.

Normally, direct and indirect tax income are used by the government to cover its costs. When expenditure increases and it becomes more challenging to raise money through taxes, governments frequently turn to public borrowing or money printing to make up budget shortfalls. Increased income tax rates have a detrimental effect on tax evasion as well as the incentives to work more, save more money, and invest more. The Laffer curve theory also shows that increasing a tax's rate over a particular point decreases revenue collection. As a result, there are limitations on increasing revenue collection to pay for increasing government spending. A budget deficit, also known as a fiscal deficit in recent years, is the outcome of the government's inability to completely finance its increased expenditure through regular taxes as a result of this resource deficiency. As a result, the government's financial limitations are reflected in the budget or fiscal deficit.

8.2. Government budget constraint

The most common expression of a government budget restriction is written as

$$G = T + AB + AM \quad \quad (1)$$

In this scenario, G stands for government expenditure (including subsidies and interest on previous debt), T for tax revenue, AB for new market borrowing (via the sale of bonds or securities), and AM for freshly minted money to fund government spending.

The government's yearly costs can be covered by tax income (T), additional borrowing (AB) from the market (both domestically and internationally), through the sale of its bonds, and by issuing new, highly-potent money (AM), also known as money financing, according to the budget constraint equation (1). You may rewrite the calculation for a budget restriction as

$$G - T = AB + AM \quad \quad (2)$$

The government must borrow more money (AB) to cover the budget deficit, also known as the fiscal deficit. To achieve this, the government must issue bonds and create new, very powerful currency (AM), also known as money financing. Thus,

Deficit in the budget= New Borrowing (i.e., sale of Bonds) + Printed Money

Either the government can create money to fund the fiscal deficit (a practise known as seigniorage) or the public (which includes insurance companies, banks, and other financial institutions) can buy bonds from the government, increasing the total amount of public debt. When bonds or securities expire, the government must repay the principal borrowed plus interest on an annual basis.

During periods of recessionary conditions that emerge from a shortage of aggregate demand, J.M. Keynes argued for the implementation of a deliberate strategy of constructing a budget deficit to get rid of recession and restore full-employment equilibrium. Recent years have seen a lot of debate among economists on the best strategies to finance budget deficits and their consequences. Budget deficits have been consistently high year after year, not only in developed countries like the United States but also in developing countries like India, which has resulted in an increasing burden of public debt and inflation, respectively. As a result, it is critical to discuss the effects of budget deficits and how they are financed.

8.3. Money financing of budget deficit

As was already noted, the government has the ability to print large amounts of money to finance deficit expenditures. Seigniorage is another term for the income generated by the creation of money. When the government creates extra money to make up its budget deficit, there are two ways to look at how this may impact inflation.

Through Money Financing, the central bank purchases assets or bonds issued by the government in order to finance government spending. To fund the purchase, the central bank issues additional money, increasing the amount of money available in the economy. The term "monetizing the debt" is used here.

According to the Keynesian view, when the money supply is increased during a depression when labour and productive capacity are idle because there is insufficient aggregate demand, the price level is unlikely to rise significantly and the result of the increase in money supply is to increase production or income. A growth in real income will boost tax revenue given the tax rate, which will normally lead to a short-term decrease in the budget deficit. However, if the economy is at or close to full employment, printing money to pay the deficit will result in inflation. Because the government may get resources by printing money, which causes inflation and reduces the real worth of the public's money holdings, doing so to cover a budget deficit that causes inflation is comparable to taxing inflation.

In order to establish a demand shortfall and a high rate of resource unemployment when the economy is in a recession, the Keynesian model adopts a fixed price level. Let's start by discussing this concept. The budget deficit (BD), where G is government expenditure, is calculated as BD=G—t(Y), where t is the tax rate, Y is real income, and T is the total amount of tax collections. (i)

Budget deficit is going to be zero and the budget will be balanced if G—t(Y)=0.

If G—t(Y) > 0 there will be budget deficit.

The short run macro equilibrium can be expressed as follows if the government funds its deficit by creating new money:

Y= Y(G, M)   (ii)

The short-run equilibrium of the straightforward IS-LM model is shown in the accompanying Fig., where the IS and LM curves converge at point E to yield the equilibrium income Yo and equilibrium interest rate r0.

In this equilibrium, if the government has a budget deficit, $G - t(Y) > 0$. In addition, the government creates large amounts of money to offset this budget deficit. The LM curve shifts to the right to the new point LMi as a result of an increase in the money supply in the economy. The figure shows that as a consequence, the equilibrium income amount increases to Yi and the interest rate lowers to ri. Assuming a sluggish economy, a rise in demand resulting from an expansion in the money supply won't raise prices.

Fig 8.1: The Impact of a Budget Deficit Funded by Money Printing, IS-LM Model.

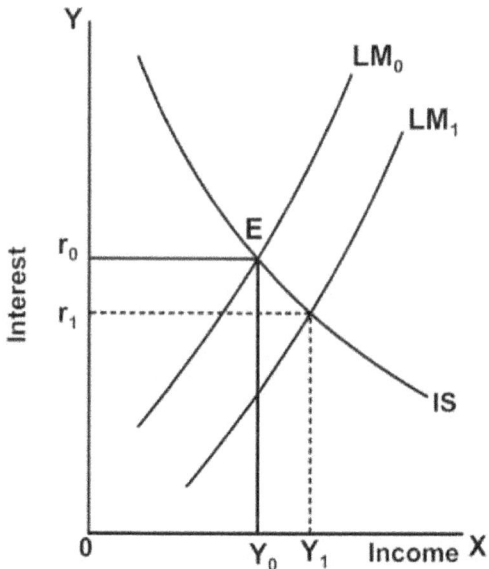

8.4. Printed money and the inflation tax

As a result of the aforementioned, inflation will happen if the economy is experiencing full employment, the GNP is expanding faster than it is, or both. According to some economists, inflationary funding through the production of high-powered money serves as an alternative to explicit taxation. Despite being a minor source of income in the majority of industrialised economies, including the US, the creation of high-powered money or inflationary financing of budget deficits has been a significant source of raising income to finance government expenditures in other countries, including India. The Central Government of India employed a method known as "deficit financing" prior to March 1997 in order to raise funds to close the budget gap. For the government, this was a substantial source of income throughout the 1960s, 1970s, and 1980s. Inflation has historically been referred to anytime new high-powered money is issued or a deficit is financed, even if it is not fully correct to state that paying for government spending by issuing new high-powered money invariably produces inflation.

Why the creation of strong money is the purpose of inflation tax, which serves as an alternative to explicit taxation as a means of paying government expenditures. With the money it prints, the government makes purchases to cover its yearly deficit. The population now has more money available to them, some of which they will save and some of which they will spend on goods and services. As a result, the government is able to buy more products and services.

The value of people's real cash amounts has decreased due to inflation, nevertheless. Specifically, utilising the funds on hand. Inflation may force individuals to buy less goods and services. When the government issues new, highly valued currency to offset its budget deficit, inflation results, which simultaneously reduces the purchasing power of the public's old money balances. As a result, inflation caused by the creation of new money is comparable to a tax on saving money. Although it may seem as though there is no tax on inflation, consumers do pay a price for inflation in the form of a reduction in their capacity to buy goods and services. According to Dornbusch and Fischer, inflation acts exactly like a tax since consumers are motivated to spend less than their income and give the government the difference in return for additional money. As a result, the government is able to spend more money while collecting less revenue from the general populace than it otherwise would. When the government funds its deficit by printing money that the public adds to its holdings of nominal balances to maintain the constant value of money balances, we refer to this as the government supporting itself through the inflation tax.

Even more specifically, we can figure out how much money the inflation tax brings in by doing the following: Revenue from the inflation tax is equal to the inflation tax multiplied by the actual monetary base.

Remember that the monetary basis is an accurate representation of the whole quantity of high-powered money. It should be mentioned that the 1980s saw a significant rate of inflation in Latin American nations as a result of the overproduction of high-powered money. As a result, a sizable amount of money was raised through an inflation tax. In fact, certain countries in Latin America struggled with hyperinflation. Thus, from 1983 to 1988, Argentina's average annual inflation rate was 359%, whereas it was 1,797% in Bolivia, 341% in Brazil, 87% in Mexico, and 382% in Peru.

8.4.1. Inflation tax revenue:

Latin American governments raised huge sums of money through taxing and the printing of a lot of money due to the high rates of inflation and regular budget deficits. The aforementioned equation shows that the inflation rate and the real money base are both necessary for the government to earn money through taxes on inflation. When the inflation rate is zero, there will be no tax income for the government. As inflation increases, so does the revenue that the government receives through taxes on inflation. However, when inflation rates increase, people tend to keep smaller real money balances as their assets' buying power declines. As a result, the public has less money and banks' surplus reserves decline as inflation rises. As a result, the public's and banks' actual money balances drop to the point where the government starts to get less money via inflation taxes. The AA curve in the following shows how the amount of taxes collected by the government changes when the rate of inflation rises.

Figure: 8.2 Inflation Tax Revenue

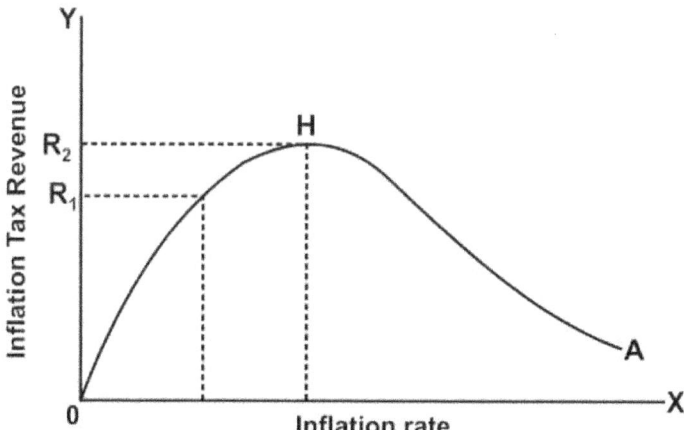

Since there is no budget deficit at first, there is no need to create money. The economy is in an initial state of equilibrium since both the inflation rate and the government's revenue from inflation taxes are zero. Now, assuming that the government decreases taxes while keeping expenditure flat, a budget deficit results, which is resolved by printing a lot more money. Additionally, the government will get tax income equal to OR if the inflation rate that arises is n. The inflation rate, however, becomes higher as more money is printed, increasing tax revenue until the inflation rate n * is attained. The amount of additional money created to fuel inflation has led to an OR2 increase in tax revenue for the government. Tax income is decreased as a result of the decline in real money balances with the general public and banks, in addition to this expansion of newly created money and an increase in inflation rates over n *. Thus, OR2 is the greatest amount of tax revenue the government may get from an inflation tax, and n* is the associated inflation rate.

Because the actual money base is relatively small in highly industrialised countries, the government only collects a little amount of money through the inflation tax. For instance, the government only receives 0.3% of GDP in taxes on inflation, or a 5% inflation rate, in the United States, while the money base only makes up around 6% of GDP. However, certain developing nations, such as Argentina. Brazil, Mexico, and Peru collected inflation tax revenues ranging from 3.5% to 5.2% of the GDP. They had to pay a heavy price for it, though, in the shape of a very high inflation rate. According to Dornbusch, Fischer, and Starts, governments get more revenue from inflation in nations with less established banking systems and big currency holdings, and thus are more inclined to give the revenue components of inflation significant weight when determining policy. In situations of extreme inflation where the conventional tax system is unable to function, the government may resort to using the inflation tax revenue as a last option. The inflation tax, however, would surely spiral out of control if it is employed frequently.

8.4.2. Evaluation of Inflation Tax Revenue:

In the study of tax income owing to inflation shown above, it is presumptive that any increase in the quantity of printed money results in inflation. We think that this is untrue. When the economy is functioning significantly below its greatest output capacity due to a lack of aggregate demand, as is the situation during recessions and depressions, the government can create additional money to finance its programmes. The resulting increase in demand would help to better use idle manufacturing capacity and give unemployed labourers work. Inflation won't come from this since more products and services will be created to meet the rising demand. In his analysis of the situation, J.M. Keynes favoured adjusting the budget deficit to fight the slump and paying for it with newly created funds without causing inflation. When the economy is experiencing full employment, the government cannot issue money to support expenditures without causing inflation.'

Similar to this, when economies in emerging countries like India continue to commercialise and see yearly GDP growth, there is an increase in the demand for money. The Indian economy also under- or over-utilizes a significant portion of its resource base. As a result, it is feasible to create enough money to cover the government's investment expenditures without causing inflation, a practise known as deficit financing prior to 1997. Therefore, it is false that inflation always happens when utilising created money to support government spending.

8.5. Debt financing of budget deficit

Debt financing involves the government issuing bonds or other securities in order to borrow money from investors to pay for its expenditures. As a result, the government now owes more money, which must be returned with interest over time. Debt financing may have a long-term impact on the economy since it pushes out private investment and slows economic growth. High amounts of government debt can also increase interest rates.

It is more typical to finance budget deficits by borrowing from the government, which then issues bonds and sells them to the general public. The general public is often not directly offered interest-bearing bonds; instead, financial intermediaries like banks do this. Using the public's monetary deposits, banks buy the government-issued bonds. Consequently, financing a budget deficit with bonds is another name for financing a budget deficit through debt. The government is able to raise expenditure while simultaneously adding to the national debt by utilising the borrowed money in this way, which has both short- and long-term effects. It should be made clear that tax reductions that keep government expenditure at the same level lead to budget deficits as well. This form of budget imbalance may also be funded via bank or public bond issuance to raise funds. The government is expected to return the principle amount borrowed in addition to the annual interest payments on borrowed funds, which might result in future tax increases.

The inflationary effects of funding a budget deficit or government expenditure have been highlighted by Keynesians. The aggregate expenditure (C+ I+ G) curve in the Keynesian model with a fixed price level rises upward when government spending is raised using borrowed money. If the economy is functioning at a level of national income below full employment and there is an output gap, the increase in debt-financed government expenditure will lead to an increase in output or income. The budget deficit will ultimately be reduced or even eliminated as a consequence of the rise in tax revenue brought on by an increase in income at the designated tax rate, putting the budget into balance. The IS-LM model may also be used to explain this, as seen in the graph below. When constructing the LM and IS curves,

Figure :8.3 Effect of an increase in government spending that was financed by debt.

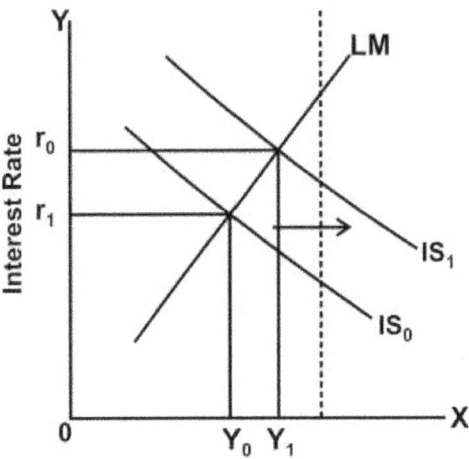

National Income

The production at full employment, given the available economic money, is Y*. At income level Yo, the equilibrium is initially reached. Due to the debt-financed rise in government expenditure, the IS curve now moves from ISo to ISi while the LM curve stays the same. As may be seen in Fig., this causes national revenue to increase to Yi.

This will lead to an increase in tax income for the government, which will eventually cause the budget deficit to reduce or disappear. It is evident from the top figure. The increase in government expenditure that is backed by debt has an expansionary impact, even when the interest rate is also rising.

However, critics have pointed out that government expenditure financed by debt is more than countered by the crowding-out effect of debt financing on private investment. The impact of crowding out on private investment can take many different forms. First, it has been shown that borrowing by the government to close its budget deficit will raise interest rates and cause a surge in the demand for lendable funds. As interest rates increase, private investment will decline. Decreased private investment results from an increase in government spending that was financed by debt. According to this argument, a rise in government expenditure has less of a net expansionary effect since it discourages private investment. On the other side, society will be compelled to shoulder the burden of growing public debt as a result of an increase in government spending that is supported by debt. Tax cuts that result in a budget deficit while maintaining the same level of government expenditure would raise interest rates, which will have the effect of discouraging private investment. Tax reductions encourage people to spend more on consumption, which decreases savings, which is why this happens. As savings decline, interest rates rise and private investment declines.

8.6. Wealth Effect of Debt-Financing

The wealth effect of debt financing was not taken into account in the aforementioned study. When the government issues bonds to cover its budget deficit, it produces private wealth. This is because people consider bonds to be a type of wealth. The money demand functions of Patinkin and Friedman's models take wealth into consideration. They assert that, in addition to other factors, the wealth's true worth has an impact on the desire for money. When the wealth effect of financing the budget deficit with bonds is taken into account, it significantly affects the dynamic behaviour of the economy. When the government issues and sells more bonds to finance the budget deficit, which will raise demand for money, the wealth of the public increases. As seen in the accompanying Figure, the LM curve moves from LM0 to LMT when money demand increases and money supply remains constant.8.4 (Note that the LM curve has dropped downward as a result of the government funding its expenses by printing money.

Figure: 8.4 Debt financing of Budget deficit with wealth effect of bonds sold by the government.

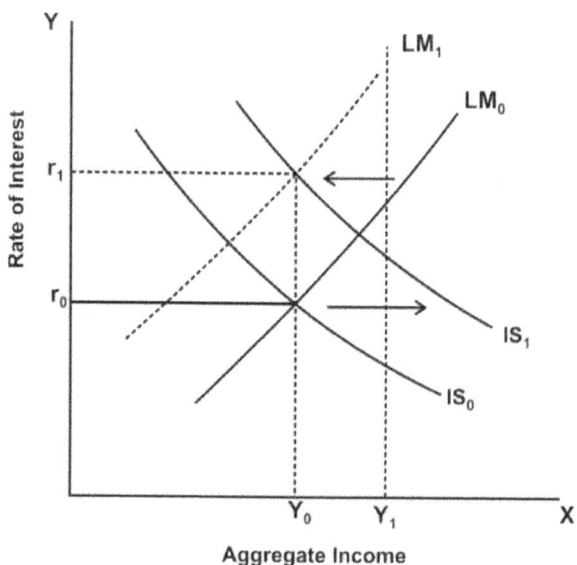

Aggregate Income

While the increase in governmental spending causes the IS curse to shift to the right to the new position ISn, which tends to raise aggregate income, the wealth effect of the bonds issued to finance the deficit causes a leftward shift in the LM curve, which tends to raise interest rates and discourage private investment. According to Friedman, the wealth impact completely negates the expansionary consequences of growing government expenditure. The preceding graph's initial equilibrium is at income level Yo. With a rise in government expenditure funded by bonds, the wealth effect causes the LM curve to move leftward to LMi and the IS curve to shift from ISo to ISi. As can be seen, the level of revenue at YO remains unchanged as a result of the increase in interest rates from RO to RI. The contractionary consequences of the debt-financed fiscal deficit are completely offset by the decline in private investment brought on by the increase in interest rates. Continued budget deficits and rising debt have led to an untenable level of debt.

Figure:9.5. Rise in price level offsets the expansionary effect of debt financing of budget deficit.

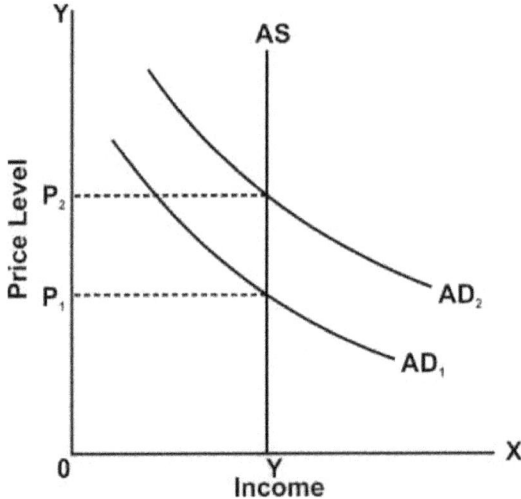

In the preceding estimate of the crowding-out impact of debt financing, the price level is assumed to remain constant. When the aggregate supply function is vertical, as it is when the economy is operating at full capacity output (i.e., full employment level), as shown by the AS-AD model in the above Figure, a rise in aggregate demand (AD) brought on by an increase in government spending that is debt-financed will result in an increase in price level, but equilibrium income will remain unchanged. Since income won't change, neither will tax revenue; as a result, the budget deficit and debt will persist over time, eventually becoming untenable.

The crowding-out effect of a debt-financed budget deficit has been utilised to counteract its expansionary impacts, as we saw above. But in our judgement, the effect of debt financing on crowding out has been greatly overestimated. In reality, debt financing a budget deficit has a negligible crowding-out impact, especially when the economy is functioning at an income level below full employment. It is often recommended to establish a budget deficit and fund it through the issuing of floating-rate bonds to battle depression when there is an equilibrium of underemployment and an output gap as a result. Furthermore, empirical evidence shows that the wealth effect of bond sales is negligible. Additionally, as will be covered in more depth further below, budget deficit policies and debt financing are efficient tools for improving economic development and income levels even in developing nations where resources are wildly underutilised or where employees are not working to their full potential.

8.7. Debt-financing of budget deficit: the view of Ricardian equivalence

a school of economics that holds that even when the government borrows more money from the people through debt, demand doesn't alter. This is due to the fact that individuals will save their additional money to cover tax increases that will be put in place later to pay off the debt. This theory was developed in the nineteenth century by David Ricardo, but Harvard professor Robert Barro would build on Ricardo's ideas to develop more nuanced interpretations of the same notion. also known as the "Barro-Ricardo equivalence proposition""

The key element of Ricardo's theory is that demand won't change regardless of a government's choice to finance expenditures with debt or taxes. The main criticisms of Ricardo's theory focus on the irrational premises that support it, such as the assumptions of flawless capital markets, the freedom of borrowing and saving, and the assumption that people will be willing to save for a future tax increase even though they may not see it in their lifetimes. Furthermore, Keynesian economics' more commonly accepted theories are at conflict with Ricardo's argument.

We've already looked at the conventional Keynesian notion of financing the budget deficit using debt. As was already indicated, when the government cuts taxes without increasing expenditure or when it raises taxes without decreasing spending, a budget imbalance may result. A more recent alternative perspective on the effects of a debt-financed budget deficit is Ricardian Equivalence, which was initially put out by David Ricardo but has since been rediscovered and enhanced by several modern economists. According to this point of view, consumers are future-oriented and base their decisions on their consumption expenditures not only on their present disposable income but also on expected future income. This concept of the forward-thinking consumer serves as the foundation for post-Keynesian consumption models like as Milton Friedman's permanent income consumption theory and Modigliani's life-saving model. When a consumer considers the future, they see the government borrowing money to close the budget gap and think that someday taxes will need to go up to repay the debt and interest. Therefore, consumers feel that the present tax cut, which causes a budget deficit that is supported by debt (i.e., the issue of bonds), boosts their income only fleetingly since their income would unavoidably drop in the future by the imposition of higher taxes to pay off the debt. As a result, despite the tax reduction and current budget deficit being funded by debt, their lifelong or permanent income does not grow. Because of this, consumers who plan ahead do not believe that the present tax cut has helped their condition and instead maintain their current level of spending and saving. In his article, Mankiw explains this concept further, stating that "the forward-looking consumer understands the government borrowing today means higher taxes in the future." Government tax cuts supported by debt just reschedule taxes as opposed to decreasing them. It shouldn't thus encourage the customer to make more purchases.

This means that consumers who are foresighted or forward-thinking will base their purchases not just on their present income but also on their lifetime income, which consists of both their current income and expected future earnings. They see government debt taken out to sustain budget deficits as being similar to future taxes since the debt incurred in the current year will be repaid by levying higher taxes in the future. Therefore, for consumers looking to the future, future taxes are identical to present taxes. Because David Ricardo was the one who first put out the idea that government debt is equal to future taxes, this concept is known as Ricardian equivalence.

The concept of Ricardian equivalence states that people's current expenditure won't be affected by a tax cut paid with debt. To paraphrase Mankiw once more, Ricardian equivalence implies that a tax cut financed with debt has no effect on consumption. In order to pay the increased taxes that the tax decrease implies, families save aside the extra cash they have available. The increase in personal savings perfectly offsets the decrease in communal savings. National saving, which was formed by combining private and public saving, stays the same. As a result, none of the effects that traditional analysis projected are produced by the tax cut.

The Ricardian equivalence concludes that a debt-financed tax cut does not lead to an increase in consumer expenditure, which in turn has no impact on aggregate demand. The debt-financed tax cut will therefore be unable to stimulate the economy.

8.7.1 Robert Barro and Ricardian Equivalence

Robert Barro, a distinguished American economist, presents an alternative explanation of the Ricardian equivalence. He further argues that debt-financed tax cuts do not raise consumer spending, negating their ability to stimulate the economy. He falsely assumes that everyone has flawless vision of the future. Furthermore, because they care about the welfare of both current and future generations equally, they do not overlook the future. In other words, in his eyes, the grandchildren and children of the current generation are the generations to come. It is wrong to think of them as independent or separate economic agents as a result. He argues that the majority of people give their children gifts, typically in the form of bequests at the time of their deaths, as proof that the current generation is just as concerned about the coming generation as it is about its own. People are not prepared to enhance their spending at the expense of their progeny, according to study on bequests. He sees everyone as a part of an eternal family. Therefore, while a debt-financed tax reduction may raise an individual's income today or over the course of their career, it won't always raise their family's income in the long run. Instead of spending the extra money he has received as a consequence of the tax decrease, he chooses to save it so that his children would be in charge of paying any further tax liabilities. Thus, it is evident that consumer spending does not increase, proving that this aspect of economic stimulation is not taking place.

The aforementioned implies that the impact of government debt depends on the people's purchasing patterns. The current evidence, however, only slenderly supports the Ricardian equivalence theory. The effectiveness of tax cuts in stimulating the economy has been evaluated in a number of economies, including the US economy. President Reagan and President Kennedy both reduced taxes in 1964 to help the American economy. The outcome was an increase in the national debt, but the American economy rebounded and came out of the previous recession. The Keynesian standard interpretation is supported by these real tests, which disprove the Ricardian equivalence hypothesis. By lowering taxes and selling bonds to close the budget deficit, President George W. Bush just made another effort to strengthen the American economy in the year 2000. This time around, it went quite well, and by the end of 2003, the American economy was back on track.

8.8. Questions

1. Explain how money supply by the government help to finance deficit budget of the country.

2. Discuss in detail borrowings by the government as debt financing of budget deficit.

3. Explain the Ricardian view of debt financing of budget deficit.

Chapter 9

Behavioural Economics and Macro Economics

9.1. Meaning and definition

The study of the influence of psychology on individual or household behaviour is known as Behavioural economics. It emphasizes on how individual or household are not always rational, that they have biases and prejudices that affect their judgment, and that their inclinations influence their decisions. Behavioural economics is broadly accepted as a way of thinking about economic issues. As per Richard Thaler, that there is a change of mind within the economics profession on the need to allow for departures from the paradigm of the "homo economicus".

Behavioural economics, on the other hand, is a branch of research that says that when it comes to making business decisions, people aren't nearly as rational as the conventional economic theory suggests. Behavioural economics provides some fascinating portrayals and explanations for individual or household interested in how sentiments and inclinations impact share prices. Arbitrage restrictions (when dealing with incompetent markets) and cognitive psychology are the two cornerstones of Behavioural economics (the way people think).

Behavioural economics and macroeconomics are two complementary subfields to each other but they having different focuses and methods. Behavioural economics focuses on understanding how individuals and organizations make economic decisions in real-world situations, considering cognitive biases, social norms, and emotions. Behavioural economics draws on insights from psychology, sociology, and neuroscience to provide a more realistic view of human behaviour than the traditional rational actor model used in classical economics.

Macroeconomics is concerned with understanding the behaviour of the economy as a whole, including economic growth, inflation, unemployment, and the role of government policies. Macroeconomics uses various mathematical models and empirical analysis to study aggregate economy.

9.2. Importance

The distinction between assumptions for productive, normal financial investment Behavioural and actual Behavioural economics is clarified by Behavioural economics. Integrating Behavioural economics into their training is critical for enhancing the customer experience, strengthening relationships, retaining consumers, and maybe delivering better outcomes.

Mindfulness, inclination, commitment, and backing are the four main categories of customer behaviour. Each of these phases is critical for the marketer.

Behavioural economics is concerned with how all types of financial investors, from ordinary individuals to professional investors, make decisions, and it encompasses all aspects of the financial industry (annuities, protection, capital, and currency markets).

Through Behavioural Economics, we can understand how people make decisions, policymakers, businesses, and individuals can contribute for good social equality and Economic stability.

Following are the economist given more contribution in Behavioural Economics:

Daniel Kahneman is a Nobel laureate and he has given contribution as a one of the founders of the field of behavioural economics. He has focused on cognitive biases, decision-making under uncertainty, and prospect theory.

Amos Tversky contributed to the development of prospect theory and his research also focused on heuristics and cognitive biases.

Richard Thaler is another Nobel laureate and he has given more contribution in the field of behavioural economics. He has focused on individuals deviate from rational decision-making and its impact on suboptimal outcomes.

Cass Sunstein is a behavioural economist and legal scholar and who has emphasis on how behavioural economics can contribute in policy design.

Sendhil Mullainathan is a behavioural economist and he has given more focus on poverty, discrimination, and decision-making under scarcity.

9.3. Key concepts

Traditional Economics & Financial Theory

Let's start with standard financial theory to better understand Behavioural economics.

The following convictions are included in conventional finance:

- The stock market and financial investors are both calm.
- Practical features are important to financial investors.
- Financial investors are very poised.
- They are not swayed by missteps in psychology or errors in data preparation.
- Theory of Behavioural economics
- Behavioural economics has the following characteristics:
- Financial investors are viewed as though they "should be anticipated," rather than as "objective" investors.
- They have discretionary cut-off points.
- Their preferences have an influence on financial investment.
- Financial investors make mental errors that lead to poor decisions.

The issue with traditional financial theories is that they only work in a perfect world! The underlying suspicions are that the data available is of high quality, and that financial investors can analyze it. Another possibility is that there is a single correct solution that can be mathematically calculated. In any case, financial investors will be disappointed if they use this concept to trade today's reality. In reality, financial markets are driven by emotions rather than prudence. At this point, the study of social finance becomes arguably the most important aspect. According to several studies, the difference between successful and ineffective financial investors is their Behavioural abilities, not their intellectual abilities.

9.4. Advantages of Behavioural Economics

Behavioural Economics is combines insights from neuroscience, psychology and economics which help to every individual in decision-making process. Following are the advantages of Behavioural Economics.

Enhanced understanding of decision-making: Behavioural economics provides insight to understanding of how people make decisions. It distinguished that people are not always rational and many cognitive biases and heuristics that can influence decision-making.

Perfect policy design: Behavioural economics help to understand how people actually make decisions; policymakers can design good policies that take into account the actual behaviour of individuals.

Efficient Economic Models: As per Traditional economic theory, it assumes that individuals are perfectly rational and always act in their own best interest. But as per behavioural economics theory, it assumes that people are not always rational and that their decisions depend on psychological and social factors.

Formulate Business Strategy: Through understanding the irrationalities and biases which affects on consumer behaviour, businesses can formulate best marketing strategies and product offerings.

Individual Development: Through understanding own cognitive biases every individual can explore more choices and avoid mistakes which is happen do to various biases

Explains Wealth as a Function of Decision Making:

Most financial investors accept that they will not make a fortune in the stock and securities market because they are not highly qualified. These people are often doctors and engineers who are well-versed in their fields, but will think less about finance in general. Thus, they take financial decisions with caution. In Behavioural economics, the key to success in the securities market is to deal with one's emotions instead of being a monetary master. Despite the fact that many inept financial investors make more money than inept finance professionals, this explains why so many finance professionals struggle in the business world.

Theory vs. Application:

According to traditional economics & finance, stock exchanges are viewed from a hypothetical perspective. Markets should function numerically if one understands traditional financial theory. Anyhow, markets will generally function as democratic machines in general. The market as a whole will be unreasonable if most members behave nonsensically for some time. Financial investors who are informed about Behavioural economics are able to identify blemishes in considering different investors and avoid committing those mistakes themselves.

Explains Asset Bubbles:

Traditional economics & financial theories have been unable to explain resource bubbles. How is it that markets continue unreasonably for so long if all members are level-headed? Occasionally, individuals value organizations higher than the whole company! Behavioural economics acknowledges that many investors aren't sure what they're doing. Sometimes they simply follow group behaviour, and this causes resource bubbles. Although traditional finance theory cannot clarify the existence of resource bubbles, Behavioural economics can. Resource bubbles occur from time to time, and Behavioural economics is the only hypothesis that can explain them, which gives financial investors more data.

Creates Buy and Sell Opportunities:

Financial investors and economist who do not recognize the Behavioural aspects of finance are also likely to follow the pattern indiscriminately. Thus, they are likely to sell when the economy is slumping and buy when it is booming. With Behavioural economics knowledge, investors can isolate calamitous events from overcompensations on the lookout. Consequently, Behavioural economics information helps financial investors to distinguish between purchasing and selling opportunities. As a result of this information, they are encouraged to deal with their feelings and think clearly, which ultimately results in more riches.

Makes Patterns Predictable:

The study of Behavioural economics reveals that people behave predictably. Emotions drive this behaviour. In the event that there is a trend in the market that promotes dread, individuals are likely to sell their stocks more often. Furthermore, when the value reaches a specific limit, there is a certain amount of bounce back. When dealing with Behavioural financial products, investors outline strategies and conduct a specialized examination to identify trends. Seeing examples of rehashing can help them make more money and increase cash flow.

Helps to Understand the Concept of Time Horizon:

Students of Behavioural economics comprehend that investors behave in different ways depending on what stage of their lives they are in. Youngsters who have quite a bit to contribute still have a lot of challenges ahead of them.

Conversely, more seasoned individuals will sell their homes when their value drops. Thus, the segment profile of financial investors also influences their behaviour. It allows them to make more precise expectations when they study segment profiles.

There are numerous wonders in the business sector that traditional financial theory cannot explain. Considering the Behavioural angles that influence dynamic, financial investors should likewise consider these angles. Markets are driven by human behaviour, no matter how silly it may seem! In denying current reality and focusing only on a desire for advancement, investors will undoubtedly make the wrong choices if they accept the universe of monetary speculations when there is abundant information, and everyone has the same cost of capital.

9.5. Criticisms

Potential reactions to Behavioural economics analysis: Behavioural economics aspect analysis has tended to focus on ideological trepidations, evidence-based trepidations, and practical issues with practical application in public administration (Puce, 2019).

The lack of a coherent hypothesis in social economics has been criticized for having such a wide range of models and absence of a unified rationale (Fudenberg, 2006). It cites that Behavioural economics contains a wide array of expectations; conflicting models and hypotheses are identifying with similar marvel and a lack of rules determining when each model should be applied. There are alternate extremes observed in Behavioural economics, and it is difficult to identify which of the repudiating tendencies is prevailing. For instance, are individuals more affected by what they saw first ("preparing" or "securing" impact) or what they saw last ("recency" impact) (Smets, 2018). According to Rubinstein (2006), conventional financial hypotheses lack style and consensus. There is no question, however, that it can be reacted to in various ways. As a collection of connected hypotheses, social economics is somewhat "a collection of devices or thoughts" (Camerer and Loewenstein, 2004). However, it is understandable and satisfiable as various economic models are suitable for different individuals in different circumstances (Wilkinson and Klaes, 2018). Science is rife with opposing theories about similar marvels, and ideological clashes usually persist for a long time. Since social economics is still in its infancy, some speculations will grow dim because of the absence of assistance, while others will be strengthened and adjusted (Wilkinson and Klaes, 2018).

Research in social economics is scrutinized by evidence wary criticism:

Broad trial research is likely to have methodological shortcomings and possibly exaggerated claims. A few early Behavioural economic experimenters like Kahneman and Tversky, who would assess hypothetical decision concentrates, need to motivate their participants to give honest, thoughtful reactions so that it is possible that the observed peculiarities may actually be ancient rarities (Angner and Loewenstein, 2012). In trials, criticism is given to potential contrasts between speculative decisions and genuine Trials have been criticized for potential contrasts between speculative decision making and actual result decisions, as well as changes in monetary motivations (Parco, Rapoport, and Stein, 2002; Holt and Laury, 200. Research facilities may not be able to apply the noticed Behavioural and result results to the analyses of certain motivating forces. Cause enduring monetary ramifications for members. In light of this criticism, it is absurd to sum up outcomes from research facility examinations to the present economic reality.

Practical Application in Public Procedures:

Criticism has been raised towards the danger that if prodding is acknowledged as an arrangement apparatus addressing unassuming paternalism, meddlesome intercessions addressing more paternalistic approaches, later on, will follow (this is the so called "elusive incline" criticism in Thaler and Sunsteins wording; Thaler and Sunstein, 2008). Strategists are viewed as facing a danger that securing individuals from their mistakes will eventually go from effectively avoidable coordinated decision engineering to expensive decision engineering or even restricting the financial outflow of legislatively coordinated ways for financial retribution. The concern is that "the wolf of hard paternalism may show up in the garments of delicate paternalist sheep" (Angner, 2016). What is viewed as a danger is additionally that acknowledgment of pushing in open approach will decrease openings to settle on choices without help from anyone else (Jespersen, 2018). Heightening of the state intercession is viewed as a danger.

9.6. Biases in Behavioural economics

9.6.1 Meaning and Importance

Behavioural economics views financial investors as "typical" but dependent on dynamic inclinations and mistakes. Dynamic predispositions and mistakes can at the very least be divided into four containers.

Self-deception: The concept of self-double dealing breaks down the way we learn. Our erroneous belief that we understand more than we do usually cause us to overlook crucial information that we need to make an educated choice.

(Investigative) Heuristic Simplification: We can also investigate a container that is often referred to as heuristic disentanglement. The notion of heuristic disentanglement refers to data preparation errors.

Feeling is a Behavioural economics container that indicates that we settle on choices based on our current emotional state. This may result in a deviation from normal reasoning.

The social container refers to how we are affected by others in our dynamic.

9.6.2 Key concepts:

Behavioural economics seeks to understand the impact of individual preferences on financial investment. Here's a list of common financial biases:

Overconfidence and the illusion of control: this is a tendency to have a false and deceitful assessment of our talents, acumen, or aptitude. So, it's a selfish belief that we're better than we are. It's a dangerous habit, but it's very profitable in the Behavioural economics and capital markets industries.

Self-Serving Bias: In Behavioural economics, there is a tendency to attribute good outcomes to our skill and bad ones to pure karma. To put it another way, we choose how to explain a result based on what makes us appear the best. Positively, a substantial number of us may look back on things we've done and conclude that when things go as planned; it's because of our skill. When things don't go as planned, it's evident that we've just experienced tragedy.

The misconception that one "generally knew" that they were accurate subsequently is known as hindsight bias. Someone may also mistakenly believe that they have a superior knowledge or ability to predict an outcome. This proclivity is a key concept in Behavioural economics theory.

Individuals' tendency to pay great attention to facts that supports their beliefs while ignoring data that contradicts them is known as confirmation bias. This is a kind of proclivity studied in Behavioural economics. In general, our preferences will limit our ability to make completely rational financial decisions.

The Narrative Fallacy: We romanticise stories and allow our need for a good narrative to obscure present reality and our ability to make objective decisions.

This means that we may be tempted to a less appealing outcome just because it has a better tale. In Behavioural economics, this is a crucial concept.

Representativeness when the similarity of articles or events confounds people's thinking about the probability of an outcome, it's called a heuristic. People have a terrible tendency to assume that two similar items or events are more closely linked than they are. This criterion of representativeness is a common data preparation error in Behavioural economics theory.

Framing Bias occurs when people make decisions based on how information is presented rather than on the facts themselves. Individuals might be influenced by similar facts presented in two different ways to make differing conclusions or choices. In Behavioural economics, investors may react to a certain opportunity in an unanticipated way, depending on how it is presented to them.

Anchoring Bias occurs when people make decisions based mostly on earlier data or main data. For example, if you initially see a $1,200 shirt and then see a $100 shirt, you're more likely to deem the to-be clothing modest. If you'd simply seen the following shirt, which is believed to cost $100, you'd probably not think it was modest. The anchor the most important value you observed had an undue influence on your evaluation. In behavioural economics, securing inclination is a crucial concept.

Misfortune Repugnance: In behavioural economics, misfortune repugnance is a tendency in which financial investors are so unfortunate of misfortunes that they focus on attempting to avoid a misfortune rather than making gains. The more misfortunes one encounters, the more likely they are to develop misfortune revulsion. Investors feel the agony of a disaster more than twice as strongly as they experience the delight of generating a profit, according to research on misfortune aversion.

Group Attitude Inclination: In Behavioural economics, group attitude inclination refers to financial investors' propensity to copy and repeat what other financial investors are doing. Rather than being impacted by their own investigation, they are often affected by their feelings and senses. As part of the Behavioural economics concept, this tutorial shows how a financial investor may succumb to group predisposition.

9.7. Questions

1. What are the differences between Behavioural economics and macroeconomics?
2. Explain the meaning of Behavioural economics and its biases.
3. Explain the importance and objectives of Behavioural Economics.
4. Explain the importance and limitations of Behavioural Economics.

Chapter 10

Caselet

10.1. Financial Crises in Yemen

Yemen is a part of Western Asia, and it is an oldest country with good historical background but Economic crises began in 2011 and it lead to increase conflict in industry, unemployment, political instability and social unrest.

The Central Bank of Yemen has been facing problem to maintain stability in the country's currency, the Yemeni rial, which has experienced significant devaluation since the crisis began. Its lead to increase inflation and also decline in the purchasing power of Yemenis and people also facing problem to afford basic goods and services.

In Yemen, Oil and Gas industry majorly contributed to exports and government revenue but due to conflict in the industry and the closure of borders export and import trade affected severely. GDP has decline by 6.7% in 2020. Due to slow down in the industry many Yemenis facing poverty and they are unable to purchase basic necessities.

Major reason of financial crises and slow down in economy is collapse of oil and Gas industry, diminution of foreign reserve and devaluation of the Yemeni rial. And these financial crises lead to increase unemployment and poverty. Yemenis not able to access basic need such as food, water and healthcare.

Due to political instability in the country international community unable provide major financial support but still international community trying to support Yemen to reduce poverty and conflict among the country. Financial crises lead to reduce National Income of Yemen and it has also affected on overall economic activities and impacted on Oil and Gas Industry, manufacturing and Agriculture sector. According to World Bank Yemen is included in low Income country group and its Gross National Income (GNI) per capita of US$ 790 in 2019.

Yemen's unemployment rate has increased after economic crises and accordingly World Bank data in 2019 unemployment rate is 22.8% in 2019. People lost their jobs due to financial crises and disruption of Investment and Trade. According to the World Bank, US$ 6.8 billion External debt was estimated in 2020 and Country's GDP was 5.5%.

Finally, to reduce economic problems Yemen has to concentrate on Political Stability, Economic diversification, Good Governance, International Trade and relations, dispute settlement between the industries.

10.2. Financial crisis in Lebanon

Lebanon country is a located in the Middle East. Roman Empire ruled in Lebanon for several centuries and after that it is part of the Byzantine Empire. In the 7th century, Due to Arab Muslim forces this country becomes a part of the Islamic caliphate. After World War I, French ruled and in 1943 they become an independent. Due to long Civil War during 1975 to 1990, Lebanon faced number of problems including regional conflicts, Economic instability and political corruption.

Financial crisis has started in Lebanon since from 2019 due to impact of Syrian civil war, mismanagement, political instability and corruption. Lebanese pound devalued by 90% against US dollar since 2019 and it led increase inflation. Banking sector also faced slowdown due to NPA loans, liquidity shortage and capital flights. Lebanon having highest debt-to-GDP ratios in the world that is more than 170% of GDP and due to this government unable to clear debt obligation. Since august 2020, Lebanon is without government after the resignation of Prime Minister. Overall external debt has increased, and it leads to devalued Lebanese pound against other currency.

Lebanese people struggling to access basic things like food, medicine and fuel. As per World Bank, unemployment rate has increased 17% to 25.4% in 2020 and specifically youth unemployment rate is 42% in 2020. GDP has declined by 20.3% in 2020. Gross National Income down from $14.1 billion to $10.8 billion 2020. COVID-19 pandemic also impacted on Banking and other Sector.

Economics crisis also led to increase Inflation, poverty rate. Service sector like banking and finance, retail, telecommunications and tourism are the largest contributed to GDP of the Lebanon but entire service sector is collapse. Construction, manufacturing, and energy sector also suffered, and Agriculture sector also affected badly.

10.3. Economic crisis in Greece

Since from 8th century Greece known for their achievement in science, art, philosophy and architecture. Ottoman Empire ruled in Greece from 1453 for more than 400 years. In the year 1821 Greece become an independent Nation.

Economic crisis has started in Greece since from 2008 due to high budget deficit, weak banking sector, large public debt and uncompetitive economy. Due to government overspending, tax evasion and corruption country's debt to GDP ratio is more than 100%. And because of overspending by government budget deficit has increased and it leads to increase country's public debt. Weak banking sector also responsible for Economic crisis and because of high level nonperforming loans (NPA) bank is unable to provide money to business and consumers.

Greece economy unable to compete with other countries economy because of uncompetitive economy includes less productivity, high labour cost and nonperformer public sector. Euro zone membership decision also not works in the favour of Greece economy because country was unable to boost exports and economic growth. Corruption, Weak Institutions and Economic imbalance also lead to increase crisis in economy.

Since from 2001, GDP and National Income of the Greece is highly fluctuated. Unemployment rate is also high that is nearly 15.5% is in 2023 but it was 28% in the year 2013. Greece received bailout packages from European Union and IMF to implement new policy in economy but still Greece having challenges in term of employment, social welfare and economic growth. Apart from this Greece facing challenges related to social inequality, refugee crisis and Brain drain.

World Bank and International Monetary Fund provided lot of financial assistance to Greece, and which is $55 billion between the years 2010 to 2015. European Union also provided financial assistance more than $300 billion over the period.

10.4. Economic slowdown in Russia

The economy of Russia is one of the largest in the world, with a GDP of approximately $1.7 trillion in 2021. Russia is a member of the G20 group of the world's largest economies and has vast natural resources, including oil, natural gas, timber, and precious metals.

Russia's economy is heavily reliant on its energy sector, which accounts for a significant portion of the country's exports and government revenue. In addition to energy, Russia also has a strong industrial sector, including manufacturing, transportation, and construction.

In recent years, Russia has made efforts to diversify its economy by promoting sectors such as technology, agriculture, and tourism. The country has also been working to increase its trade relations with other countries, particularly those in Asia.

Overall, the economy of Russia remains an important player in the global economy, with both challenges and opportunities for growth and development.

According to the World Bank, the International Monetary Fund (IMF) and the Organization for Economic Cooperation and Development (OECD), 2022 was a bad year for the Russian economy. It is estimated that in 2022, Russia's gross domestic product (GDP) dropped by 2.1%.

Russia's economy may continue to shrink in 2023. Its GDP is forecast to decline by 2.5% in the worst-case scenario (OECD) or by 0.2% according to the World Bank. The IMF expects growth in 2023 (0.7%).

The restrictive measures target the import of certain goods from Russia and the export of certain goods to Russia. The list of banned products is designed to maximize the negative impact of the sanctions on the Russian economy while limiting the consequences for EU businesses and citizens.

According to the International Energy Agency, Russia's oil revenues dropped by over a quarter in January 2023 (compared to January 2022). The drop in February was even more significant (over 40%).

Some of the major reasons economic crisis are Economic dependence on natural resources, Weaknesses in the banking sector characterized by weak regulation, poor governance, and a lack of transparency, Political instability, Economic sanctions imposed by Western countries, Fiscal policy and external debt etc.

10.5. Economic crisis in Zambia

Zambia is a developing country with a mixed economy, with both private and state-owned enterprises. The country has a relatively small economy with a gross domestic product (GDP) of approximately $23 billion in 2020, according to the World Bank. Zambia's economy is heavily dependent on the mining sector, particularly copper, which accounts for over 70% of the country's export earnings. Other minerals such as cobalt, gold, and zinc are also important exports.

Despite its rich natural resources, Zambia remains one of the poorest countries in the world, with high levels of poverty and unemployment. The country has also been affected by a significant amount of external debt, which has hindered its economic growth and development.

Zambia has been experiencing a financial crisis in recent years, characterized by high inflation, a weakening currency, and a growing public debt burden. The country's debt-to-GDP ratio has risen rapidly in recent years, reaching around 120% in 2020, up from around 60% in 2015, according to the World Bank.

The Zambian government has been struggling to service its debt obligations, leading to a default on its sovereign debt in November 2020. The government has since been negotiating with its creditors to restructure its debt, but progress has been slow.

Zambia's financial crises have been caused by a combination of factors, including external debt, dependence on copper, poor governance, political instability, currency depreciation, and the impact of the COVID-19 pandemic.

The financial crisis has had severe consequences for the Zambian people, with high inflation leading to a sharp rise in the cost of living and reduced access to basic goods and services. Unemployment has also risen, and the crisis has put pressure on the government to cut spending on critical social services such as health and education.

Unemployment has been a persistent challenge in Zambia, with the country's unemployment rate averaging around 13% in recent years. However, the COVID-19 pandemic has had a significant impact on the Zambian labour market, with unemployment rates increasing to an estimated 22% in 2020.

10.6. Economic crisis in Suriname

Suriname is a country located in South America in north-eastern region. Suriname economy is depending on export of natural resources like oil, gold and bauxite. This country is famous for rainforests and its cover 90% area of land. Suriname combines elements of Dutch, Indian, African and Indonesian culture.

After COVID 19 pandemic, reduce demand for exports and decline in commodity prices and its lead to increase Economic slowdown. Suriname is the poorest countries in South America. Suriname faces social and political issues, including inequality and corruption. The country has a high poverty rate, and many people unable to access basic services such as healthcare and education.

According to the World Bank, Suriname's Gross Domestic Product (GDP) was approximately 3.3 billion USD in 2020. Suriname's economy is dependent on the extraction and export of natural resources, particularly bauxite, gold, and oil. Country faces several challenges, including high levels of debt, inflation, and a shortage of foreign exchange.

According to the World Bank, Suriname's Gross National Income (GNI) per capita was approximately 5,670 USD in 2020. Suriname's total debt was around 128% of the Country's GDP. And to reduce the high debt levels, the Surinamese government has implemented a range of fiscal reforms, including efforts to reduce spending, improve tax collection, and attract foreign investment.

World Bank approved US$ 40 Million loan in 2020 to improve health care system, social assistance and expansion in economy. In 2021, IMF made agreement of US$ 690 million economic program to support in tax administration, investment promotion and public financial management.

Suriname faces a range of economic challenges, including high levels of debt, limited foreign investment, and a reliance on commodity exports. To reduce challenges will require a range of solutions, including:

Diversification in Economy: Along with oil, gold and bauxite sector government must work to diversify the economy by promoting sectors such as agriculture, tourism, and manufacturing.

Encouraging foreign investment: Suriname can attract FDI in sectors such as mining, energy, and infrastructure. The government should provide favourable investment climate by implementing policies that promote transparency, stability, and predictability for investors.

10.7. Economic crisis in Sri Lanka

Sri Lanka is a small island nation in South Asia. In 2018, Sri Lanka faced a debt crisis as external debt increased rapidly, and the government unable to repay its debts. This led to a currency crisis, with the Sri Lankan rupee devaluated against the US dollar. And to correct it government cutting public spending and increasing taxes.

Despite these challenges, Sri Lanka continued to experience economic growth in recent years, with GDP growth of 2.3% in 2019 driven by strong growth in the services and industrial sectors. However, inflation remained high, reaching over 6% in 2019.

Sri Lanka's economy was also impacted by causes from the outside world, including as the COVID-19 pandemic. Because of the impact that the pandemic had on tourism as well as other industries, the country's economy shrank by 3.6% in the year 2020. In order to provide support for the economy, the government enacted several methods of economic stimulation, such as lowering interest rates and providing financial help to enterprises.

The economy of Sri Lanka is facing challenges in the areas of managing its weight of debt, lowering inflation, and encouraging economic growth that is sustainable. The government has stated that it is dedicated to carrying out ongoing economic reforms in order to solve these difficulties and foster economic growth over the long term.

Managing the debt can be accomplished through boosting tax collection, decreasing government spending, and negotiating debt restructuring agreements with creditors. These are some of the potential methods that can be implemented to solve these difficulties. The government could also pursue measures to limit inflation, such as raising interest rates, slowing the expansion of the money supply, and fostering more price stability. These are some examples of possible policies. Implementing structural reforms, expanding economic diversity, fostering regional collaboration, and providing support for entrepreneurial endeavours and innovation are some further potential options.

The realization of every economic reform initiative is contingent on a number of elements, including political will, the participation of stakeholders, and efficient implementation.

Sri Lanka is confronted with a number of economic difficulties, any one of which could be addressed using one of several potential solutions. These possible answers are as follows:

1. Debt management: Sri Lanka is able to focus on managing its debt burden by implementing a combination of initiatives. These include boosting revenue collection, decreasing government spending, and negotiating debt restructuring agreements with creditors.

2. Control of inflation: The government has the ability to enact policies to reduce inflation, such as raising interest rates, slowing the expansion of the money supply, and fostering more price stability.

3. Implementation of structural reforms: Sri Lanka has the potential to improve the productivity and level of competition in important facets of the country's economy, including agriculture, industry, and tourism, by putting in place structural reforms. As part of these reforms, improvements might be made to the infrastructure, investments could be made in education and training, and corporate entrance obstacles could be lowered.

4. Diversification: Sri Lanka's economy might benefit from being diversified by the introduction of new sectors and the expansion of those that already exist. For instance, the nation might encourage the growth of renewable energy, information technology, and high-tech manufacturing industries.

5. Cooperation with neighbouring regions: Sri Lanka might aim to develop regional economic cooperation with its neighbours, such as India and China, to encourage trade and investment flows and to enhance economic integration. This would be in an effort to increase economic integration.

6. The encouragement of entrepreneurship and innovation: Sri Lanka may place a stronger emphasis on the encouragement of entrepreneurship and innovation by offering assistance to small and medium-sized businesses and start-ups, as well as by encouraging a bigger investment from the private sector in research and development.

The successful implementation of these solutions is contingent on a number of elements, including political will, engagement from relevant stakeholders, and efficient implementation. The success of any effort to reform the economic system is dependent not only on the aforementioned aspects but also on the economic and political environment in which these solutions are put into practice.

10.8. Conclusion

There are various causes of economic failure like geopolitical conflicts, pandemics, natural disasters, corruption, political instability, ineffective institutions, Inefficient and outdated industries, inadequate infrastructure, changes in global market, fluctuations in commodity prices, demographic factors and monetary and fiscal policies of the particular nations. Along with this various Economic shocks, Bad governance, structural problem and external factors are also affecting of entire economy. And all these factors lead to increase inflation in the country, high unemployment rate, depreciation of currency, down fall in GDP and National Income, high poverty rate and inequality in economy and society.

Every nation is working for economic welfare, and they have to consider following factors and different ways for overall economic development.

- Organized Macroeconomic framework
- Favourable Business environment
- Encouragement for Innovation and New Technology
- Infrastructure assistance
- Assistance for International Trade and Exchange
- Equality and Social inclusion
- Best Educational system and Investment in Human Capital

GDP (Gross Domestic Product) and National Income is a key indicator of every economy, so government has to provide assistance through following different ways to increase National Income and GDP.

- Foreign and Domestic Investment
- Encouragement of Entrepreneurship
- Boost Export Trade
- Promote Research and Development Activities
- Improvement in Infrastructure
- Reduce external Debt
- Better taxation policy

Macroeconomics provides border views to policymakers and analysts to identify key trends, challenges, and opportunities for economic development. Macroeconomic theory provides a framework for developing policies to enhance economic growth, reduce unemployment, and stability in prices. Macroeconomic indicators such as GDP, inflation, and unemployment rates provide a basis for measuring economic performance, identifying areas of strength and weakness, and tracking progress over time.

At the end macroeconomics is a crucial subject in economic development because it provides a framework for understanding the behaviour of the economy as a whole and developing policies to promote sustainable economic growth and development.

Suggested Readings / References

Edward Shapiro, Macroeconomic Analysis, Fifth Edition, 1984

M C Vaish, Macroeconomic Theory, Thirteenth Edition, 2007

H.L. Ahuja, Macroeconomics Theory and Policy, Twentieth Edition, 2019

N. Gregory Mankiw, Macroeconomics, Tenth Edition, 2019

V.K. Puri, S.K.Mishra & Bharat Garg, Fortieth Edition, 2022

Apostolakis and Viskadouraki (2017), Analysis of the economic impact of cultural festivals in the local economy, Cultural Management: Science and Education, Volume 1 (2017), Issue No. 2, pp.47-64

Economo, F., & Philippas, A. K. (2010). An Examination of Herd Behavior in Four Mediterranean Stock Markets. 9th Annual Conference Proceedings. Athens: Europian Economic and Finance Society.

Herbert, A. S. (1979). Rational Decision Making in Business Organisations. The American Economic Review, 69(4), 493-513.

www.ingramcontent.com/pod-product-compliance
Lightning Source LLC
LaVergne TN
LVHW061547070526
838199LV00077B/6938